THE YOUNG

AN APPROACH FOR TEACHERS
AND STUDENTS

JOAN LAST

Second Edition

OXFORD   NEW YORK

OXFORD UNIVERSITY PRESS

Oxford University Press, Walton Street, Oxford OX2 6DP

Oxford New York Toronto
Delhi Bombay Calcutta Madras Karachi
Petaling Jaya Singapore Hong Kong Tokyo
Nairobi Dar es Salaam Cape Town
Melbourne Auckland

and associated companies in
Berlin Ibadan

Oxford is a trade mark of Oxford University Press

Published in the United States
by Oxford University Press, New York ·

First Published 1954
Second Edition 1972
Fourth impression revised 1978
Ninth impression 1990

ISBN 0–19–322287 6

Printed in Great Britain by
Halstan & Co. Ltd.,
Amersham, Bucks

CONTENTS

ILLUSTRATIONS

AUTHOR'S FOREWORD

THIS book is primarily concerned with the first few years of piano-playing. It contains no complicated or advanced theories, and nothing that cannot easily be understood by all who read it. It is intended to serve as a guide to young students, or teachers gaining their first experience of teaching, and also contains suggestions which may be helpful to teachers of longer standing.

My first aim is to make the young pianist into an 'artist in miniature', and even the earliest lessons can be directed towards this ideal. Thus, Part III, 'From Student to Artist', may be said to embody the main theme of the book, with Parts I and II as essential towards its fulfilment.

There is a degree of attainment which, though it is only relative, can be reached in every grade, from the lowest to the highest. The performance of the very simplest music can be stamped with the hall-mark of the embryonic artist, and give real pleasure, both to performer and listener.

It is of the greatest importance not to try to go too fast. Simple music played beautifully is more satisfying than difficult music played badly. There are no easy ways and short cuts to real piano-playing and, if one has any hope for the young pianist's future, one must set a high standard from the start.

The teacher of the beginner carries a big responsibility and should be as highly trained as the teacher of the more advanced pupil; but academic qualifications are not enough. The successful teacher sets out to understand the limitations of each pupil and approach every one as an individual. This understanding, allied to an untiring patience and a sense of humour, are the human qualifications required.

This book, then, contains suggestions which should help the teacher towards these ideals. The very earliest stages are dealt with in minutest detail, because they are the foundations upon which all that follows will be built. Many Professors of Music think of Grade I Associated Board Examination as being for beginners, but it is far from it. Many stages of progress are passed and a great deal has to be taught and assimilated before the pupil reaches Grade I, or, let us say, before the pupil can tackle Grade I pieces with understanding and some artistry.

No one is infallible. Teachers are always, in the end, the learners. Fresh ideas and methods are propounded almost daily, but one fact remains. It is, that music is an art, and the piano a means of expressing that art. The pianist seeks to perfect his control of the instrument that he may use it as a medium of artistic expression, not as a mere exhibition of 'key pushing'.

To this end the teacher of the beginner lays the foundations for the pianist and musician of tomorrow.

Notes

Throughout this book the teacher is referred to as 'she' and the pupil as 'he' for the sake of clarity.

It has not been possible, in a book of this kind, to give many musical illustrations, but further examples of exercises, sight-reading and pieces &c., will be found in several books of music for the pupil which I have written on the lines suggested here, entitled *At the Keyboard* and *Freedom Technique*. English terminology is used for the naming of time values. American readers should refer to the table on page 68.

Note on the Second Edition

I have been wanting for some years to re-write certain parts of this book. I am grateful for the opportunity to do so. I have tried to bring the music lists up to date and also to clarify some points about technique, particularly the section about 'Staccato'. Other small alterations are the inevitable result of several more years of teaching and thinking.

January 1972

Note on the 1978 impression
Once more I have to thank the publishers for giving me the opportunity to read and re-assess certain passages in this book. The basic ingredients are much the same, with minor alterations. However, new ideas on the subject of Interval Recognition (page 61) and Rhythmic playing (pages 73 and 74) may interest those who are familiar with previous editions. Music lists are difficult to compile due to the ever changing scene in the publishing world but I have done my best to offer a limited amount of help in this direction.

J.L.

ACKNOWLEDGEMENTS

I should like to thank all my friends and pupils, whose interest and encouragement have prompted me to write this book, and also Rosalind Ryton for her helpful suggestions, Joan Lawrence for her assistance in preparing the typescript, and Sonia and Christopher Copeland for so patiently posing for the photographs.

The photographs are by J. White and Son, Littlehampton.

The passage from Debussy's *Children's Corner* is quoted by permission of Durand et Cie.

January 1954

J. L.

Part One

THE BEGINNER

INTRODUCTION TO PART ONE

THE art of piano-teaching has been completely revolution-ized during the past fifty years and many outstanding books have been written on the subject. These I do not seek to supersede. Instead I have aimed at bringing all the material for the first lessons down to what might be called the 'bare bones'. I have described in the simplest possible way a sug-gested course for beginners which I have found successful, hoping that it may be of use to teachers who find the first lessons of all the most difficult part of the whole business.

With all deference to the writers of books on teaching, particularly on the technical side, I feel that many of them have never dealt with the very small beginner, and most of their theories cannot be put into practice until many of the stages covered by this book are passed.

In writing the following chapters I have in mind children aged between six and eleven years. On the whole, seven and a half seems a good average age to begin the piano, but, of course, this varies considerably according to the mental and musical growth of the child.

Very young beginners, of five years or under, sometimes appear to make remarkable progress at first, and can be taught up to a point by imitation or 'rote'. A large part of their lesson is taken up with rhythmic training and singing. In actual piano-playing they progress a certain way and then appear to stand still and, very often, to lose interest. This is because, though musical ability may be there, the sense of application is not sufficiently developed to take the child beyond a certain point. It is often found best to discontinue lessons for a while until interest is re-awakened. In this case the parents should watch the child's reactions and see whether he goes voluntarily to the piano, or shows disappoint-ment that there are no lessons. If the obvious desire to continue is there, then it would be a pity to stop the lessons, and the teacher will have to try to introduce as much variety as she can into them.

With the average child, however, it can be said that this early start is a mistake, for he will have progressed no further at the age of ten or eleven than he would have done if beginning lessons at seven or eight.

These remarks do not include children of really exceptional talent, whose musicianship and brain are far beyond their years. They are, at an early age, capable of making quite startling progress and maintaining it.

Nine- and ten-year-old beginners usually get on quickly, but it is better to begin lessons, if possible, not later than eleven. During the years that follow there is often a reticence and lack of confidence which hinder progress. Suitable music is hard to find, as the 'teen-ager' does not approve of being given the pieces which are written for young children, and yet cannot manage the things which appeal to him. An inferiority complex often results, and the older beginner refuses to practise if anyone is within earshot. Naturally there are always exceptions—those, for instance, who have been longing to learn the piano ever since they can remember, and, at last, have been given the opportunity. To them the beginner stages are only a means to an end, and they are completely oblivious to what anyone thinks about their practising. Their greatest wish has been granted, and they will do everything in their power to make up for lost time. What a joy these enthusiasts are to the teacher, who number among them not only those in their teens, but mothers, fathers, and even grandparents!

This brings me to the subject of parents. What a help *or* a hindrance they can be! On the whole, one can breathe more easily when the pupils have their lessons at boarding-school and are not expected to be able to produce almost miraculous results from each lesson. By the end of the term even the very slowest will have something to show. One

PLATE I

Fig. 1.—Position of hand on keyboard

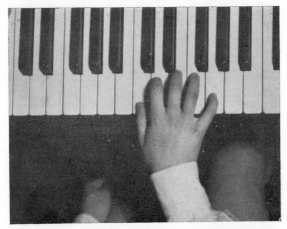

Fig. 2.—Position of hand (from above)

PLATE II

Fig. 1.—The 'float off' after the 'Run and Jump' Exercise. (This is the same as for the slur)

Fig. 2.—Preparation for Sixths Exercise (or any chord) played with arm-weight

Fig. 3.—The relaxed arm

must, however, always remember that it is the parents who are paying for the lessons and hoping to see results, and they have every right to know what is going on. The trouble is that the teacher very often does not know what is 'going on' at home. The piano may be out of tune or almost unplayable whilst the room has the added attraction of television. The family, probably, will grumble or criticise, or a shy, and not very capable child, is made to show 'what he can do' to friends and relations. No wonder progress is sometimes slow and the pupil discouraged. Ideally the piano should be in a room apart from family activities.

Often one sees an advertisement such as: 'Piano, suit learner, £40' but, in fact, the beginner, above all else, needs a reasonably good instrument if he is to become sensitive to tonal control. Some mothers have a leaning towards a new, shiny piano to tone with the room, yet many of the most suitable instruments are those of sound 'pedigree' that have been reconditioned by a reputable firm. To choose a piano should be left to someone knowledgeable who can vet the instrument *inside*, ensuring a touch that is not too heavy for small fingers and a tone that is pleasing and flexible in its variety. Harsh tone or inadequate tuning will, in time, blunt the most sensitive ear. Finally, where no practising facilities are available the teacher should refuse the pupil. Nothing but frustration can come from such a situation.

The teacher will say that it is not for her to push her way into the home and interfere with domestic matters, or dictate to the parents. I am not suggesting that she should actually do that, but, in view of the fact that the parents have selected her to teach the child, and are obviously anxious for progress to be made, it would be wise to intimate to them in the first place the conditions conducive to the best results, rather than to wait until the parents complain that the child is not getting on as well as they had hoped.

In the case of smaller children the co-operation of the parents is essential. It is a good plan for the mother to attend an occasional lesson to see how the child should sit, and to get an idea of the work that is being done. These attendances should not be too frequent, as children are usually much easier to teach when mother is not there. She can also have quite a paralysing effect upon the child by chipping in at intervals during the lesson with such remarks as 'He could play it perfectly well at home', or (to the child), 'There, you see, I told you you were doing it all wrong'.

Then there are the few enthusiasts amongst parents who take lessons themselves, sometimes for their own pleasure, but often to keep *au fait* with the teacher's methods and to be able to help the child. This is a wonderful idea unless (as is not unlikely) child outstrips parent!

What we have to remember is, that all parents are anxious for the children to make progress, and none of them would willingly put any obstacle in the way of this progress; therefore it is for the teacher to make her wishes clear from the start, and to have as close an understanding with the parents as possible.

THE FIRST LESSON

ONE cannot lay down the law as to how the first lesson should be conducted. Whatever method is preferred (and there are a variety of excellent ones), there still remains the fact that no two pupils are alike, or can be taught on exactly the same pattern. Much depends on the age, ability, and attitude of the pupil. Most children will arrive full of enthusiasm, their fingers itching to get at the keys and their one idea to learn all they can. A few may be unresponsive and apparently have little interest, though this attitude, more often than not, is due to shyness. Those who are antagonistic to the whole idea are, fortunately, a thing of the past. Gone are the days when the young lady of education learnt the piano as a matter of course. Few present-day parents will arrange lessons for the child who has no inclination for music.

Normally the young beginner likes to settle down to the keyboard as quickly as possible, but the hesitant or shy child need not be hurried, and will probably respond better if a large part of the lesson is taken up with talking about music in general, comparing different instruments and the way the sound is produced, or discussing the musical activities with which the child is already familiar at school, such as the Singing Class or Percussion Band. In any case, all pupils will be interested in 'how the sound is made', and should be shown the inside of the piano and given a simple explanation of the working of the key, hammers, and dampers. A main point to stress is the fact that the quality and quantity of tone can be varied according to the way in which the key is struck, and this should form a basis for the first lessons on the keyboard.

Again we have to consider the very young beginner, the child who is still almost a baby. Though, as I have already said, it is usually wiser not to commence lessons too early, yet there are some parents who are anxious that it should be given a trial, and, provided they understand that progress in actual piano-playing must inevitably be slow, quite a lot of musical experience and enjoyment can be had from these early lessons. Here the teacher must realize that the child is too young to be made to concentrate, and often, when in the middle of explaining something, and, as she imagines, holding the child's attention, a small voice will interrupt with: 'Do you know, we've got a puppy at home', or (implying that the teacher's efforts are not very impressive), 'My mummy can PLAY the piano'. On one occasion, after carefully drawing what I thought was a beautiful treble clef, I heard a rather scornful voice remarking: 'My daddy can draw a *crocodile*'. After that it was rather difficult to come down to such mundane things as treble clefs! However, it is all fun, and, provided the parent does not expect to see a great deal of progress *at the piano*, the foundations for a musical understanding can be laid. Rhythmic exercises, including clapping or other movement, are always enjoyed. Songs and little 'guessing games' should be included. The 'guessing games' are, of course, aural tests under another name, and quite a number of easy ones can be devised for the very young. The youngest pupils love to have a manuscript book, and will often fill it from cover to cover in a week. The results will be quite unintelligible, but the enthusiasm is there, and they very quickly learn how to write clefs, notes, rests, and so on.

With the exception of these very young people, the main part of the lesson is, of course, at the keyboard. This should be preceded by a short explanation of 'how the piano works', as already suggested. Having found, then, that the key can be struck a number of different ways, producing different effects, the problem is for the beginner to do this. That (it should be explained) is why pianists, however clever and famous, are always working at what is called TECHNIQUE. They must have perfect control of the instrument to play fast or slow, loud or soft, and produce all those wonderful effects which are the real art of piano-playing.

Here, then, the pupil should be seated at the piano at the correct height, so that the arm from elbow to wrist slopes neither up nor down. The arm must be lightly poised. It should support the hand, and not drag it downwards. The hand itself forms a slight uphill slope to the knuckles, curving away to the finger-tips (see Plate I, facing p. 4). It is very important not to sit too close, and, if the child's feet do not reach the floor, it is an advantage to use a footstool. Those who can reach the floor should sit slightly forward on the stool, so that a little of the weight of the legs rests upon the feet.

The distance from the piano is tested by the pupil reaching towards a very high note with the left hand and then towards a low note with the left. The time has passed when first-term pianists were restricted to a five note compass. We now encourage free movement over the keyboard from the start.[1] With those who can reach the floor make sure they sit well forward on the stool. By 'using less stool' they are able to

[1] As in Joan Last: *Freedom Technique* (O.U.P.).

swing from side to side and cover the keyboard with ease. Many Intermediate to Advanced students come to me having problems with four-octave arpeggios because they have always sat solidly, as on a chair. A simple change of position works wonders.

We are now ready, with the finger-tips resting upon the keyboard. Let the fingers be placed over a group of five notes, so that any key in the five-finger group can be pressed down without a constant readjustment of the hand (see Plate I, Fig. 2). It will be seen that the second and third fingers fall nearer the black keys, and the fifth finger near the edge of the keys. The thumb falls into a natural position on its side and should have contact with the key a little beyond the length of the nail. In all preliminary exercises this position should be adhered to as nearly as possible. So many beginners play far too near the edge of the keys, resulting in a bad jerk when the thumb comes into action, and even more serious trouble when the black keys are used.

From this position an introductory exercise can be tried. Number the fingers for the pupil from 1 (thumb) to 5. Then get him to press down any number finger you may call (helping it with a little weight from the arm), hold it down for four counts, and then release it, feeling the rebound of the key. Take each finger in turn (though not straight up from 1 to 5). Repeat the exercise, counting two for each note, or asking the pupil to experiment with different lengths of sound. During the whole time contact should be kept with the keys.

The pupil is now ready to learn the 'geography' of the keyboard. We teach D first because it is easy to locate 'between the *two* black keys'. Let him find D's all over the piano, pressing each gently with a curved 3rd finger; as he becomes confident let him 'fly' from one D to another, spanning several octaves and moving the arm freely in an arc or 'rainbow'. This free movement prevents tension which can result from constant downward pressure. Next we introduce

C and E (one on each side of D) and, again, the pupil plays these, in rising or falling sequence, at various registers. Middle C is then established and becomes the starting point for the first technical exercises. It is not essential, during the first lesson, to learn other notes, these come in the lessons that follow and the intelligent child will pick them out for himself if it is explained that music notes only go 'from A to G'.

First we teach a 'legato' exercise. The ability to play 'legato' in the first stages is important. If this is not developed, many difficulties will arise later on. We are told that legato is produced by 'transferring the weight from the bottom of one key to the bottom of the next' but, of course, such a description is too complicated for the child. A simple explanation is that it is like 'walking'. The main thing is that the pupil should be taught to *listen* and let one sound continue to sing until the next one is heard—no 'gaps' in the sound. The teacher can demonstrate legato and non-legato with the pupil listening and criticizing. See also the section on 'Legato and Finger Activity' on page 22.

During the exercise that follows, the fingers should be rounded, but not 'curled up'—the hand should be 'cupped', so that, if inverted, it could hold a ball. A small amount of arm-weight is advisable, as the fingers are not yet very strong, and in this way a singing tone can be more easily developed.

See-saw Exercise
(By rote. It is only necessary to know the locality of Middle C.)
Right Hand
(starting with Thumb)

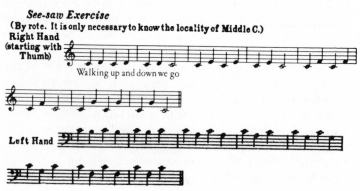

Walking up and down we go

Left Hand

It might be considered by many that it would be more ideal to begin the exercise thus:

using complete rotation from 1 to 5. Of course it can be done this way, but the very small child usually finds difficulty in using the fifth finger at first, and the effort causes stiffness; therefore I prefer, in most instances, to work up to the fifth through 2, 3, and 4.

For an older beginner it could be called a rotation exercise, and might be extended as follows:

Rotation Exercise

Next we must turn our attention to lightness of arm and ability to move freely over the keyboard. This little exercise can be tackled in the first lesson, and gives a sense of lift and easy movement:

Let the pupil accent the first note of every group and 'float off' the last note (see Plate II, Fig. 1, facing p. 5). Be careful that the phrasing is not distorted as follows:

Played in the correct manner, this makes a good preparation for staccato.

From the earliest lessons chords of some kind should be tried, to be played with arm-weight touch, and to help develop a full singing tone. All except the very weak-fingered can, at the first lesson, make some attempt at playing a progression of sixths, and they are also pleasant to the ear of the pupil. To enable the pupil to obtain the correct condition of hand and arm so as to produce this touch, it can be described to him as sinking into a nice comfortable chair. With very small children the exercise can then be called 'Chairs':

(Prepare for the next chord on the fourth beat.)

The fingers should rest on the keys in the position for playing each new chord before it is struck, then, with the fingers gripping the keys, the forearm should be relaxed slightly (see Plate II, Figs. 2 and 3, facing p. 5).

These three exercises—'Walking', 'Run and Jump', and 'Chairs'—are sufficient for the first lesson. Extensions of the same ideas will be found in the chapter on 'Early Technique' (page 21) and are implemented in *Freedom Technique* (Joan Last, O.U.P.).

The pupil should not be kept too long at the keyboard during the first lesson, and at this stage it would be a good thing to make a break and try a few aural tests. Suggestions for these, including what I have called 'Listening Tests', will be found in a later chapter. Whatever tests are given must be very easy, or the pupil will take fright and give no answers at all. Singing should not be forced if the pupil is shy about it, but small children will usually be delighted to sing you any nursery rhymes they may know, and the teacher of very young children should always have these at her finger-tips. Finishing off the last note of a tune, which can be treated as a guessing game, is surprisingly successful with less shy children, and another popular game is that in which the teacher, starting on a central note, plays a succession of notes up and down the piano, pausing after each one for the pupil to say whether it moved 'upstairs' or 'downstairs'.

The smallest pupils will by now have had nearly as much as they can manage, but would enjoy trying to play a little piece by rote before the lesson is finished. No. 1 on page 15 could be attempted, or something similar. Remarks about pieces for beginners will be found later in the book. For those who have covered the ground fairly easily up to the present, a first attempt should be made at reading the notes from the music. The method used here is to start with Middle C and work outwards. This, of course, is only one of several methods but it will be found the easiest for the young beginner to grasp.

The teacher will first draw the great stave of eleven lines, and indicate the compass on the piano which these lines cover.

Middle C →

It should be explained that music was written for voices before the piano came into existence, and that this stave covers the range of the singing voice, from the lowest man's voice to the highest boy's or woman's voice. Notes higher or lower than this on the piano have to be written on special little lines called 'leger' lines. (These will be learnt later on.) It was soon found that counting and reading from so many lines was difficult, so the stave was divided into smaller groups of five lines, or clefs. Those used for the piano are called 'treble' and 'bass'. Middle C has a little

line of its own, which is written either at the top of the bass
stave (or clef) or at the bottom of the treble stave.

For the present we will assume that the treble clef belongs
exclusively to the right hand and the bass to the left.

Having found the position of Middle C below the treble
lines, we next find D, and then E. The pupil is given a manuscript book in which these three notes are written. The
teacher then writes a line of notes similar to the following:

asking the pupil first of all to point out all the C's, then all
the D's, and finally all the E's. The next step is to play the
line of music in the right hand, commencing with the thumb
on Middle C. The same process is repeated for the first three
notes in the bass clef, i.e. Middle C and the two immediately
below. He should be encouraged to do this without looking
at his hands (certainly by the second lesson). Finally the
pupil is given a line of notes, in treble and bass, to copy and
name before the next lesson.

It will be noticed that the notes have been written as semibreves, because this gives plenty of time for thought between
each note. The name 'semibreve'[1] should be taught, and its
value. Other note-values will, of course, follow at subsequent
lessons, but, for the average child, this will usually be found
enough for one lesson.

The pupil who has some previous knowledge of notation,
or who is unusually quick, would, of course, learn more notes
at the first lesson, and could also be given simple rhythmic
tests for clapping at sight. In this case time signatures and

[1] Semibreve is the English term for a 'Whole Note' or one of four
counts. See table on page 68.

bar lines would first need explaining. The teacher should be prepared to improvise exercises to suit each beginner, as there can be no set way of teaching children of varying degrees of intelligence and ability.

Now we come to the highlight of the lesson, at least from the pupil's point of view, and that is 'The Piece'. Perhaps some readers will be surprised that I have even mentioned such a thing in connexion with the first lesson, but it must be realized that, to the child, anything is a piece that has a title, or that has words to fit the tune. A mere handful of notes that can stimulate the imagination, or paint a sound-picture, will give the greatest pleasure, and a real sense of attainment.

In a later chapter will be found illustrations and suggestions for the type of music which is suitable in the early stages, but I cannot write about the First Lesson without here including one or two examples of a First Piece. They should, of course, be taught by rote, as the few notes that can be *read* could hardly be built into anything very interesting.

The foregoing are the suggested outlines for a first lesson, which could be adapted to suit varying ages and types of pupils. On account of the detailed explanations, there may appear to be rather a lot of material, but, briefly listed, the main divisions are as follows:

1. Talk and introduction to the piano.
2. Sitting posture, position of hands, and introductory exercise.
3. Note finding on the keyboard.
4. Three little technical exercises.
5. Aural work.
6. Sight-reading.
7. A piece.

The youngest pupils may not get through all this, but the pupil of eight years or over usually covers the ground. It is, of course, more than likely that there will be some who have the greatest difficulty in finger and hand control, resulting in the stiffness which is the despair of so many teachers. There is no doubt that the child stiffens because he feels that what he is trying to do is very difficult and will require much effort and concentration. This very outlook results in stiffened muscles, and the harder he tries, the stiffer he becomes. It is therefore of the greatest importance to set the child at ease and to explain that, at first, you are only going to ask him to do things which are quite easy, until his hands and arms 'get into training'. Everything should be made to appear easy and natural. No physical action should be beyond the scope of the child's hand. If the effort appears too great and the stiffness persists, it seems better to discontinue lessons for a while, rather than lay what will eventually be the worst possible foundations.

In my examining experience I have noticed that severe problems arise where children seem to be making a continuous effort to 'push down' the keys. Piano playing requires 'exertion and release', and the moment of release is usually the more important. For this reason I would suggest that most early exercises are played gently without force and the child encouraged to move from one level of tone to another as soon as possible.

Before saying good-bye to the pupil make sure that he knows exactly what you want him to do in his practice time. Write the details and any instructions that are necessary in a notebook: tell the parents you have done this, and see that the book is always brought to the lesson.

The beginner should not practise too long at first; the set work will probably not take more than fifteen to twenty minutes. This is quite long enough for eight years and under. On the other hand, any child who enjoys sitting at the piano and picking out little tunes he has heard, or making them up, should not be discouraged or corrected, even if the technique does go somewhat astray. In our anxiety to teach all things correctly from the start we sometimes lose sight of the fact that the child wants to '*play the piano*'. The set work must, of course, be carefully done first, but after that the young artist should be free to enjoy his own music in any way he wishes.

Part Two

FROM BEGINNER TO STUDENT

INTRODUCTION TO PART TWO

IN the first part of this book I tried to collect together the material and ideas that go into the first lesson of all. In doing so I have, naturally, only touched briefly on each section, and there are many ends which must now be picked up.

The progress of each individual after the first lesson is so variable that, from now on, we cannot set down what is to be done at the second lesson, at the third, and so on. Some will develop a good natural technique but find sight-reading difficult; others will have poor finger control and be good at aural tests; there may be some who will need to go over the first beginnings several times before they are ready to go on.

This section is concerned with all stages of piano-playing from the beginner to about V or VI Associated Board, or a similar Grade. In writing about these things one cannot draw the line at any definite Grade or Stage, and it is for the teacher to take and use the material that she finds will best benefit the pupil.

EARLY TECHNIQUE

Arm Freedom

Success or failure as a pianist depends largely on the early years, when good or bad habits are being formed. One must, at all costs, train the hands and arms into good habits, so that the pupil is not constantly struggling to express himself against the handicap of a poor technique.

In describing the position of hand and arm at the first lesson I mentioned that the arm should support the hand, and not drag it downwards. This is most important, and as the repertoire increases and more speed of movement over the keyboard is needed, it is the arm that steers the hand to the required position, so that the fingers can play their part without any sense of strain. For this reason it is a good thing to give plenty of technical exercises of the kind that call for a free movement over the keyboard. The pupil might begin the lesson or practice with a progression similar to that which I called 'Run and Jump'. It is impossible to play this well with a stiff and heavy arm, and it produces the correct conditions for the freedom we require. The teacher should be continually improvising technical progressions to suit the requirements of the pupil, and the following variant of the 'Run and Jump' could be tried:

Legato and Finger Activity

The 'walking' exercise should be practised for several weeks, or a variation of it. It keeps the hand well balanced and prevents the 'falling off the keyboard' which usually occurs when the fourth and fifth are played in ordinary five-finger exercises (see Fig. 1 opposite). It is easier in the early stages to maintain a legato when a slight rotary movement is made, and it is not possible, in the 'walking' exercise, to hold down more than one note at a time. The thumb has a great deal to do in this exercise, and we must make quite sure that it is doing it the right way. Do not let the arm do all the work: *the thumb must move independently.* A simple exercise can be given for this. Let the pupil rest the four fingers on a table, or on the closed fall of the piano. He then beats out with the thumb a rhythm in crotchets and minims which the teacher has clapped. This activity of the thumb is of great importance, and, if it is achieved, we do not hear that bumpiness in scale

PLATE III

Fig. 1.—Little finger played too much on the edge, causing the hand to 'fall off' the keys

Fig. 4.—Right hand ready to begin a scale—slanting slightly across the keys

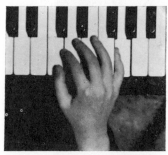

Fig. 2.—Little finger played too much on the side, and with the length of the finger in contact with the key

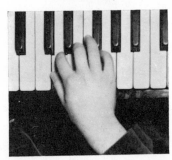

Fig. 5.—As the second finger plays the thumb prepares to go under

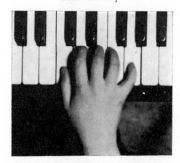

Fig. 3.—Correct way to play the little finger in simple five-finger groups

Fig. 6.—Incorrect position for thumb as second finger plays

PLATE IV

Fig. 1.—Incorrect position of body which is too rigid as right hand reaches for a high note

Fig. 2.—Correct position of body—travelling with the hand

and arpeggio passages which proclaims its use. Of course, a similar kind of exercise at the keyboard or away from it could be used to develop finger activity, but it must be remembered that the upward movement of the finger is only a preparation for the downward one, and that the fingers should never be strained upwards to a degree of discomfort.

The swing of the pendulum during the last fifty years has gone from one extreme to the other. At one time the great thing was to lift your fingers up. Everyone practised Schmitt and other exercises assiduously, and the higher the finger-lift the greater the achievement. I recently had shown me a dummy keyboard on which a block had been fixed for holding the arm, so that the fingers could be exercised with the arm absolutely rigid!

When the revolution came, and the word 'relaxation' came to the fore in connexion with pianoforte technique, there was a swing in the opposite direction, and relaxation was prac-tised to such a degree by some enthusiasts that the poor fin-gers took second place, and could do no more than waft over the keys in a vague and forlorn fashion. This, of course, happened only in extreme cases, but it certainly is true that finger-work was sadly neglected by many teachers in their efforts to be 'up to date'.

The present-day teachers strive to maintain the balance between these two extremes, and the arm, hand, and fingers each have their own particular part to play. This, to the beginner, needs to be as uncomplicated as possible. It is of no use to talk to the child about muscular activity and in-activity, co-ordination, exertion, relaxation, and so on. The very phrase 'depress the key' has an unfamiliar ring about it. It is more easily understood by the child if we say: 'Play this note, play it softly, play it loudly, make it sing for a long time, make the shortest sound you can', &c.

I want to make it clear that I am not offering any new ideas on technique, but simply trying to find a way to make things as straightforward as possible for the ordinary average child who learns the piano. The old advice: 'Lift your fingers' had at least the advantage of simplicity, whereas modern technique has become so complicated that the mere action of playing one single note would appear to be as hazardous as that of hitting a golf ball down the centre of the fairway!

Let us assume then, that the teacher feels that the pupil has learnt to play the 'walking' exercise with nicely balanced tone and hand and finger action. Now is the time to introduce a finger exercise. Mr Schmitt and others have, I am sure, exhausted all possibilities, and I cannot suggest anything new, but I do feel that the kind which progress up and down the keyboard are the best and are enjoyed the most by the pupils. This is the simplest one of all, which we all know, and which with small children I have called 'A long walk':

In playing this the pupil should listen carefully, to make sure he is producing a true legato, each sound singing on till the next one is made, but no two notes held on together. It is not always easy to get the happy medium between these two things, as the timing has to be exact. There is one moment, and one moment only, when the weight must be transferred from one finger to the next. The teacher should play the progression to the pupil, reproducing these two extremes, and then correctly, so that he can hear the difference. For the pupil who does not join the notes, and who breaks up the continuity of sound, the following exercise might be tried. Play the sequence of notes *slowly*, counting two. Each note is played on the first count, but is not released until the second count after the next note has been played. In this way each note is really held on for two beats and overlaps the next.[1] Of course, this would be the last exercise to give to a pupil who holds down more than one note at a time. This is caused by lazy finger action, and is a case where I would say: 'Lift your fingers up'. Perhaps, more correctly, I should say, 'Let the key come up', but it is questionable whether the child with untrained and insensitive fingers would really be able to respond to this suggestion as easily as to the more direct one of 'Lift your fingers up'. If it is, at the same time, explained that the finger must be lifted sufficiently to be ready to play the next key, then the process will be made clearer in the child's mind.

For those with this fault, I suggest the following simple exercise:

Place the fingers and thumb in a natural position over a five-finger group. Let these five notes then be put down. Count four. On every fourth count lift one of the fingers, and, with it, restrike the note on the first beat, holding the others down. Remember the lift always comes on four and the note is struck on one. The pupil can either go straight up and down the group of notes, or vary the order at the direction of the teacher, but it should be played rhythmically and in strict time.

The fourth and fifth fingers are, naturally, weaker than the others. The fifth finger, in particular, needs to be carefully watched, as the wrong action will cause a lot of difficulty later on. The tendency with beginners is to play it on the outside, with quite a lot of the finger lying flat on the key (see Plate III, Fig. 2, facing p. 22). To do this the pupil rotates the hand sideways, and, whilst a rotary movement is desirable in certain passages of the Broken Chord type (see Plate VI, facing p. 35), yet it is certainly not correct for all passages, and to develop the fifth finger in this way is quite wrong. The progression of sixths referred to earlier helps to strengthen the fifth finger, and makes it impossible for it to roll on to the side. But, of course, the fingers must learn

[1] The very structure of the key involves a minimal overlap in a pure legato though this is not apparent to the listener.

to work independently, and where weakness is evident exercises similar to the following can be used:

All exercises for finger agility should be practised slowly at first and with no undue arm exertion or weight. The pupil should realise it is pointless to attempt a speed beyond clarity and control.

Arm-weight and Chords (see Plate II, Figs. 2 and 3, facing p. 5)

The progression of sixths given in the first lesson should be practised daily. The full tone that it is possible to produce in this way lays the foundations for a singing tone in the future. The best results are obtained if the chords are played very slowly, with the fingers firm, and relaxation of the forearm. This must not be confused by the child with a 'collapse' of the wrist. The whole movement needs to be carefully controlled. The phrase 'sinking into a chair', which I mentioned earlier, helps to get the correct results. When the progression can be played with ease a further note might be added:

Finally, the following progression can usually be managed towards the end of the first term, unless the child has unusually small hands:

For those who have small hands, a simple exercise, in which the triad is built up note by note, would be better, and could be played in different keys to make it more interesting.

It is, of course, a good thing to combine these with a rotary exercise and, eventually, one can build up progressions combining the various aspects of technique as they are taught.

The following combination of rotary and chord technique also teaches the triad and its inversions:

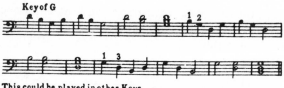

This could be played in other Keys

Staccato

The pupil who has gained technical freedom through the 'Run and Jump' exercise should have little difficulty in progressing to single staccato notes, though the technical conditions are not identical.

Theorists, quite rightly, tell us that all we have to do to play staccato is to 'cease all effort at the moment the sound is made' and to avoid all conscious (or imposed) *upward* movement after the key has been struck. This seems all very simple and succinct until you put it to a small child. 'But', he argues, 'I must take the note *up*!'. It can, of course, be explained that the key will rebound if you let it do so, but this rebound depends upon the speed with which it is depressed; therefore staccato demands a different 'attack' from legato. How confusing such explanations can be to a child. I have always found that 'word pictures' are more readily understood than 'theories'.

The pupil with a free and well supported arm is likely to respond quite naturally to a staccato direction if being told to 'hop' rather than to 'walk' (as in legato). This he does by playing a sequence of notes, or a scale, with the 3rd finger. I have also heard a suggestion that the young pianist imagines he is hitting a row of small tin-tacks into the keys; this can be demonstrated on the fall of the piano or even on a table, but insist on *small* tin-tacks, not outsize nails (!) for early staccato is better if played softly.

Many teachers liken staccato to a bouncing ball. Here the upward bounce is the *result* of the downward speed, but the child may tend to exaggerate the height. This should be avoided if possible. However, I see no reason why *all* movement should be checked, providing the wrist is neither locked nor flabby. The real danger lies in the kind of introduction to staccato that was put out in my childhood! I well remember being instructed to play a series of sixths, flinging my wrist and arm back as far as I could after striking each one, and returning to rest on the surface of the next. What frustration such a beginning caused when the time came to speed up the staccato passages. In fact, such a method cannot result in ability to play staccato at speed.

Staccato can vary from almost a 'pin-prick' of sound to detached notes of longer duration. These varieties are dictated by the context of the music and will be learnt later (see page 140). For the present we simply describe staccato as 'sounds that are not joined'. After introductory scale or five note sequences further exercises[1] could be as follows:

Hot Cakes

---

[1] For further staccato exercises, see *Freedom Technique* (Joan Last, O.U.P.).

Staccato could then be combined with finger agility exercises:

The left hand takes all the foregoing exercises at a convenient pitch. On the whole it is best to take them from the centre of the keyboard outwards.

The Slur

The slur is sadly neglected in the performances of many young pianists, and it would be better to include it in the lesson as early as possible. It is not really difficult, and the pupil usually appreciates the shading of tone and imitates it well. The very simplest of exercises can be used to introduce the slur. Let the pupil think of a 'down, up' movement, the down movement being on the first note (the strong beat), and the up movement on the second note (the weak beat).

Here is a suggested first exercise. Let the pupil imagine he is 'floating off' the second beat (see Plate II, Fig. 1):

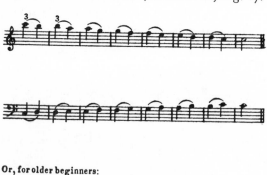

Or, for older beginners:

Later the slur might be attempted from weak to strong, and the 'Float off' becomes a 'kick off':

Exercises can be taken which combine quaver passages with slurs and staccato:

Much more will be found about the slur on pages 123–4.

Part Playing

In quite elementary pieces one will meet with this type of progression ♪♪. Simple part-playing exercises will prepare the pupil for it. They cannot, of course, be given to complete beginners, but can be taken as soon as the pupil has a good technical control over a single line of melody. These exercises have been written for the right hand, but should, of course, be taken at a suitable pitch in the left hand:

Scales and broken chords are not included here, as they are discussed from the technical point of view in the chapter on 'The Scale and Key'.[1]

[1] Extensions of all exercises given here appear in Joan Last: *Freedom Technique*, Book 1 (O.U.P.).

Recommended Books of Technique

VERY EASY

Alphabet of Exercises	Mungo Park	Forsyth
Fun Fair	Joan Last	O.U.P.
I'd like to be	Joan Last	Forsyth
Little Technics	Dorothy Bradley	Ricordi
Dozen a day	Edna-Mae Burnam	Chappell

PROGRESSIVE

Freedom Technique (Grades I–VIII 3 books)	Joan Last	O.U.P.
Musical Exercises	Walter Carroll	Forsyth
Technical Aids (Grades I–III)	Mantle Childe	O.U.P.
Pianoforte Technique in an Hour a Day	G. Tankard & E. Harrison	Novello

STUDIES

The Wheel of Progress (Graded)	Thomas Dunhill	Assoc. Board
Twelve Studies	Walter Carroll	Forsyth
London Today (based on intervals)	Joan Last	O.U.P.
Time Twisters	Joan Last	O.U.P.
Studies in Technique and Rhythm	Joan Last	M.S.M.
Studies Op. 100	Burgmuller	Prowse

(These last are suitable for 'concert performance' as, at a later stage, are the three books of studies by Heller (Galliard).

FIRST PIECES

THE writing of pieces for the young has become almost as serious an art as that of writing full-scale pianoforte works. The technique, however, is entirely different. The composer cannot let himself be carried away by heights of inspiration, but is always having to consider the Grade in which he is writing the piece. If he writes even one bar beyond the difficulty of that Grade, however effective it may appear to be, he has defeated the end which he has in view, and that bar raises its head like an evil spell every time the piece is taught. I am not suggesting that the young pianist must never be expected to tackle any difficulties, but that the grading of the pieces learnt should increase so gradually that the difficulties are never insurmountable. It is much better to teach that which is well within the grasp of the performer, so that attention can, even at an early stage, be given to the finer points of artistry, phrasing, expression, tone production, and so on. I have so often heard young pianists struggling through works which they can never hope to play within a year, by which time they are so heartily fed up that learning music becomes a drudgery, instead of the pleasure which it was intended to be.

To encourage artistry in the complete beginner, the present-day educational composer gains his effect with a mere handful of notes which are contrived to illustrate some mood or picture, or to fit the words of a rhyme. In these he incorporates some technical and musical purpose, such as the contrast of legato and staccato, the slur, accents, scale passages, broken chords, tied notes, and so on. Gone are the days when beginners ground their way through endless variations of the C to G five-finger group in the right hand, accompanied by a tonic dominant bass. What scope had these young students for artistry or imagination in performance?

There is no doubt that the present-day beginner is well catered for in this respect, and there is plenty of music from which the teacher can choose.

A piece need not necessarily be on a five-note compass to be easy. On the contrary, many so-called beginner's pieces of this type are extremely difficult. The following, for example, will present quite a problem for any pupil in the first term, and, even when learnt, has not much about it that appeals to the child:

In contrast, this two-part piece, in which the hands take it in turns to move, is much easier and more interesting:

etc.

The first pieces of all should be ones in which melodic interest is shared between the hands. One of the type here given is easier than either of the last two and usually a success during the first term:

Sailing with the Breeze

When new rhythms are introduced, pieces which have rhymes to fit the words are a great help, and much enjoyed:

Two little raindrops Said let's have a ride Down the window pane we will slide.

A simple melody in one hand, accompanied by legato chords in the other, can also be attempted, provided that the chords are placed so that the 'lift', or change of chord, coincides with a new phrase in the melody:

PLATE V

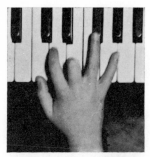

Fig. 1.—G major scale
R.H. Incorrect approach to
F sharp

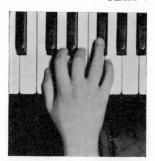

Fig. 2.—G major scale
R.H. Correct approach to
F sharp

Fig. 3.—F major scale
L.H. Incorrect approach to
B flat

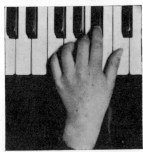

Fig. 4.—F major scale
L.H. Correct approach to
B flat

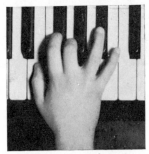

Fig. 5.—B minor scale
(harmonic)
R.H. Correct way of
playing the G

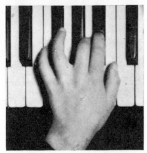

Fig. 6.—B flat minor
scale (harmonic)
L.H. Correct way of
playing the A

PLATE VI

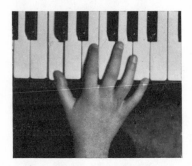

Fig. 1.—Broken chord
R.H. Thumb starts. Wrist slightly relaxed and first note accented

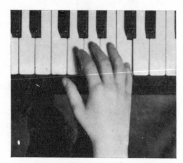

Fig. 2.—At the top
The hand is rotated towards fifth which is played lightly

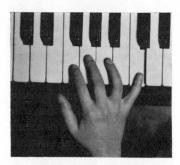

Fig. 3.—Broken chord
Descending. Weight towards the fifth finger which is accented

Fig. 4.—At the bottom
The hand is rotated towards the thumb which is played lightly

Music that moves over a large area of the keyboard but which has a pattern that can be followed at different pitches is very much easier than it appears. It should, of course, be taught by rote. Children much enjoy this kind of piece, which encourages freedom of movement over the keyboard.

The slur is a special teaching feature in this example:

The following is also easy, but too much of this sort of thing becomes dull, and does not tend to develop the imagination; it is not recommended:

Small chords are not found difficult, and an occasional sharp or flat in pieces which are taught by rote is always a great success and never forgotten by the performer, who looks upon it as a great sign of achievement. Here staccato and groups of quavers are an added feature:

Tiptoe Dance

As the pupil progresses he should be given some of the easier classics. Though simple in structure, they demand more from the performer than is often realized. Phrasing, style, balance between the hands, and good tone control are needed here, and, if a child is to play them well, much attention must first be paid to those points mentioned in Part III of this book, in the Chapters 'Common Faults, their Anticipation and Prevention', and 'The Pathway to Performance'. The teacher would be well advised to make a catalogue of suitable pieces for all Grades and styles to which to refer. This is, of course, constantly added to as new publications appear, or as she becomes acquainted with other works.

As a beginning, the following list of suggestions might be found useful to the young teacher who is beginning her career. The following selections from educational pieces are believed to be available at the time of going to press. It is understood that many other works are equally suitable.

FIRST PIECES. MOSTLY SINGLE NOTES

A Day with Peter and Penny	Joan Last	O.U.P.
Companion Pieces	Diller and Quaile	Chappell
Ever so Easy	Henry Duke	Freeman
Five Tones Five Fingers	Karl Heinz Füssl	Universal
First Album	Christine Brown	Freeman

Fun on the Piano	Gertrude Gardner	Lengnick
Folk Songs for the Piano	Sylvia Lindo	O.U.P.
Pieces to Play. Book I	Ticciati	Curwen
Pantomime Pictures	Joan Last	O.U.P.
Puck's Pieces	Joan Last	Boosey
Tune Time	Henry Duke	Freeman

FROM FIRST TERM TO GRADE I

Contrasts (4 sets)	Joan Last	Bosworth
Easy Solos for Piano	Sylvia Lindo	O.U.P.
First of all	Joan Last	Chappell
The First Concert	Joan Last	O.U.P.
Holiday Pictures	Leslie Fly	Forsyth
Leisure and Pleasure	Marjorie Helyer	Freeman
Time to Play	Janet King	M.S.M.
Summer is Here	Joan Last	M.S.M.
Party Pieces	Joan Last	O.U.P.
Pets' Corner	Eric Thiman	Ascherberg
Summer Afternoon	Helen Lockhart	Forsyth
Tom Tiddler's Tunes	Joan Last	Bosworth
Tunes for Beginners	Barbara Kirkby-Mason	Curwen

GRADE I

Country Outing	Joan Last	O.U.P.
Farmyard Parade	Joan Last	O.U.P.
Gay Pictures	Marjorie Helyer	Novello
In a Garden Gay	Joan Last	O.U.P.
Odds and Ends	Quaile and Hart	Chappell
Out and About	Henry Duke	Freeman
Sketches from Hans Andersen	Yvonne Adair	O.U.P.
Ten Little Ditties	Jessie Furze	Ascherberg
Twelve Easy Pieces	Dyson	Ass. Board
With my camera in the Country	Joan Last	Freeman
Album for Youngsters	Henry Duke	E.M.I.
Tune Time	Dorothy Parke	Roberton
The Day's Play	Joan Last	Forsyth

GRADE II

The Big Top	Joan Last	O.U.P.
By Sea and River	Joan Last	Freeman
Canterbury Tales	Leslie Fly	Forsyth
For Your Delight	Marjorie Helyer	Freeman
Four Seasons	Joan Last	M.S.M.
Forest Fantasies	Walter Carroll	**Forsyth**

Highdays and Holidays	Marjorie Helyer	Freeman
Magic Circle	Joan Last	O.U.P.
Ship Ahoy	Marjorie Helyer	Novello
Six Little Piano Pieces	Jessie Furze	Ascherberg
Spring Seranade	Joan Last	O.U.P.
Western Suite	Thos. A. Johnson	Freeman
Village Sketch Book	Cecil Baumer	Ascherberg

GRADE III

Carnival Procession	Joan Last	William Elkin
Cherry Stones	John Longmire	Freeman
Festival Suite	John Longmire	Bosworth
Five Pastels	Swinstead	Bosworth
The Pet Shop	Louise Garrow	Leeds Music
Six Gay Dances (each separately)	Joan Last	Freeman
Three Seascapes	Joan Last	O.U.P.
Zoo Pictures	Eric Thiman	Prowse
Village Pictures	Joan Last	M.S.M.

GRADE IV

Down to the Sea	Joan Last	O.U.P.
Fancy Free	Swinstead	Assoc. Board
Four Song: Without Words	Norman O'Neill	O.U.P.
Street Scenes	Eric Thiman	Prowse
Sea Idylls	Walter Carroll	Forsyth
Summer Dances	Margaret Judd	Bosworth
Tree Pictures	Joan Last	O.U.P.
Water Pieces	Eric Thiman	Prowse

CONTEMPORARY MUSIC – GRADES I to IV

Children's Piano Pieces by Soviet Composers		Boosey
Double Dozen for Small Fingers	Jeno Takacs	Universal
For Talented Beginners (two books)	Anthony Hopkins	O.U.P.
Fifteen Children's Pieces	Kabalevsky	Boosey
Five Easy Variations	Kabalevsky	Boosey
Hybrids	Ferenc Farkas	Mills Music
Les Cinq Doigts	Stravinsky	Chester
Playground	Anthony Hedges	Universal
Piano Music for Children (two books)	S. Stravinsky	Novello
Pictures of Childhood	Khachaturian	Boosey
Recipe – for a little girl	Warren Benson	Leeds Music
Six Children's Pieces	Shostakovitch	Boosey

Ten Finger Orchestra	Bernard Boldon	Hinrichsen
Thirty-two Piano Pieces	Bartók	Boosey
Mikrokosmos I–III	Bartók	Boosey
Five by Ten I–IV (British Composers)		Lengnick
Black and White	Joan Last	O.U.P.
Notes and Notions	Joan Last	O.U.P.
From Russia for Youth	ed Boris Berlin	Frederick Harris
For Children. 1 and 2	Bartók	Boosey
24 Little Pieces	Kabalevsky	Boosey
Five Piece Suite	Michael Jaques	Roberton
A Week of Birthdays	Rodney Bennett	Belwin Mills

SHORT LIST OF CLASSICAL REPERTOIRE

A Little Notebook for Anna Magdalena	Bach ed. Langrish	Assoc. Board
Six Minuets	Mozart	Assoc. Board
Six Sonatinas	Haydn	Schott
Six Sonatinas	Beethoven	Galliard
Album for the Young	Schumann	Galliard
Lyric Pieces Op 12	Grieg	Novello
Album for the Young	Tchaikovsky	

ALBUMS WITH EACH COMPOSER SEPARATE

Master Series for the Young	ed. Edwin Hughes	Schirmer
Step by Step to the Masters		Banks

ALBUMS OF GRADED CLASSICS

Selected and Graded Classics	(Grafton Edition)	Freeman
Hours with the Masters	ed. Bradley	Bosworth
Step by Step to the Classics	ed. Swinstead	Faber
Young Pianist's Repertoire	ed. Fanny Waterman	Schott
Bach to Beethoven (2 books)	ed. Rehberg	Schott
Classics to Modern		Yorktown Press

EARLY KEYBOARD MUSIC

Airs and Graces	ed. Craxton	O.U.P.
Early English Sonatinas	ed. Rowley	Boosey
Old English Worthies	ed. Rowley	Boosey
Keyboard Music from the Seventeenth Century	ed. Hans Barth	Mills Music
Eighteenth Century Clavier Pieces	ed. Kreutz	Schott
Alte Hausmusik	ed. Rehberg	Schott

SHEET MUSIC (all Grades)

The Grafton Classics	Freeman
Pleasure and Progress	Lengnick
Short Original Pieces	Assoc. Board

Sonatinas are excellent training for the works of Haydn, Mozart, and Beethoven. Those of Clementi and Kuhlau make good stepping-stones to these classical works.

THE SCALE AND KEY

THE scale has more than just a technical use, and for this reason has not been included in the chapter on early technique. However, I will deal with this side first, as a good technical foundation in scale-playing is of the utmost importance.

At whatever speed scales are played, and whether the performer is a beginner or in the Advanced Grades, the flow of notes should be as continuous and even as possible, and, to attain this, certain things must be taught correctly *from the beginning*.

It is a mistake to allow the pupil to use arm-weight touch in very early scale-playing. The energy must come from the hands and fingers, or very soon a 'pump-handle' action will result, which is very difficult indeed to stop, and makes fast scale playing an impossibility.

The turn of the thumb need not present any great difficulty. For smaller children the following introductory exercise may be taken:

Peeping Tom

The pupil should be directed to slant the hand across the keys sufficiently to allow the thumb to pass under without jerking the whole arm as it does so (see Plate III, Fig. 4, facing p. 22). The elbow should be easily balanced, and not held close to the side. This slant should, of course, not be exaggerated, but it will be noticed that scales can never be played smoothly and at speed by students who have been allowed to jerk the thumb under in the early stages.

Another important point is to see that the pupil moves the thumb close to the second finger immediately after it has played, so that it can gradually creep under and be ready for its next note. The simplest way to explain this to the child is to tell him that the thumb is travelling all the time (see Plate III, Figs. 5 and 6).

The body should not be held rigid, and this applies to all pianoforte-playing. It should move slightly with the hand and arm as they travel up and down the keys (see Plate IV, Figs. 1 and 2, facing p. 23). This may not seem necessary for scales of one octave, but I see no reason why the average pupil should not be allowed to play two octaves after a fairly short time; the technical advantage is much greater, and the sense of achievement encouraging to the young pianist.

I have already suggested that it is wise to train the fingers not to play on the edge of the keys. If scales are played on the edge of the keys there will be trouble immediately the first sharp or flat is introduced. Many new pupils have come to me knowing the notes of quite a fair number of major and minor scales, but unable to play them with any kind of continuity or flow, because of the awkward way in which they use their hands. To take the first example: The pupil is learning G major in the right hand. He reaches E with the third finger well on the edge of the key, only to find that a manœuvre as pictured in Plate V, Fig. 1, facing p. 34, is necessary to reach the F sharp. Similarly, when playing F major in the left hand, the same difficulty will arise if the third finger A is not played well forward on the key. (Plate V, Figs. 1–4, will illustrate correct and incorrect hand positions for these two scales.)

Two minor scales which present some difficulty are B and B flat minor harmonic. The cause is very similar. In each of these we have a white key lying between two black keys to be played with the third finger of each hand. In B minor the key is G, and in B flat minor it is A. This white key must be struck by the third finger on a level with the second and fourth, *not farther back*. It is difficult to explain this in words, but Plate V, Figs. 5 and 6, will illustrate.

Then we come to fingering. I do not need to tell the readers of this book that certain recognized fingering sequences exist, but only to say that, whatever method is chosen, this must be insisted upon. Thus fingering becomes a matter of 'muscular habit': as Sidney Harrison puts it; 'Your muscles must know for certain whose turn comes next'.[1] This muscular habit, or 'knowledge', means a security of direction when scales are played 'hands together'. For the purpose of fixing the fingering in the mind write special points or 'sign posts' in the pupil's notebook. The examples here are quoted for the 'Standard Fingering'.[2]

> *Scale of D major.*
> > R.H. 4th on C sharp.
> > L.H. 4th on E.
> > 3rds meet on F sharp and B.

Make sure to put the left hand 4th on E descending.

> *Scale of B flat major.*
> > R.H. 4th on all B flats except the first.
> > L.H. 4th on E flat.

Notice that they come on the opposite black keys.

> *Scale of E flat minor (harmonic).*

Watch the left hand 3rd and make sure it comes on D descending.

And so on, *ad infinitum*. We all know what are the common mistakes, and they should be anticipated, and the pupil warned beforehand.

Of course, one can buy a book of scales and arpeggios, but that is not really the best way to teach them.

A few pupils find difficulty in playing the hands quite

[1] *The Young Person's Guide to Piano Playing* (Faber).
[2] See *Associated Board Scale Books* for alternative fingerings.

together, and this will be mentioned again later in the book. The fault should never become chronic if the pupil is made to listen most carefully for it from the start.

In mentioning the technical aspect of the scale first, I feel that I may have 'put the cart before the horse'. The reason for doing this was to make a link with the earlier chapter on technique.

We now come to the most important aspect of the scale: that of understanding it as a key upon which all music is built. We are, of course, discussing the major scale to begin with. This is the one to which the ear of the average child is the most accustomed.

The scale of C is taught first, and, until this has been mastered technically, it is not necessary to teach its structure. After the pupil can play it, ask him now to begin on G and play a scale from there, making no comment on the fact that it may sound strange. Most children will notice something wrong and remark on the fact. If they make no comment the teacher will say, 'Didn't that sound as though something was wrong?' Then ask them to play it again and try and find out *which* note sounded 'wrong'. When this has been discovered (it may take one or two attempts), and the teacher has suggested the substitution of the black key above F for F, it is time to explain the structure of the scale. Tones and semitones are demonstrated (for small children I have known these to be called 'big steps' and 'little steps'), and the teacher must make sure they are clearly understood. Ask the pupil to play, for example: 'A tone above C'; 'A semitone below B'; 'A semitone above B', and so on. Now slowly play the scale of C major again, pausing after the second note: 'Was that a tone or semitone from C to D?', then after each note till the correct interval has been named. It will be found that the interval of a semitone occurs only twice—between the third and fourth notes, and between the seventh and eighth. This is important, and now we can see, by carefully playing a scale from G, why there has to be an F sharp. The next question is, 'What is a sharp?' I wonder how many young (and old) pianists of to-day would answer: 'A sharp is a black note.' Far too many, I am afraid. We must get this right once and for all, and see that the pupil is quite sure of the correct answer: 'A sharp raises a note one semitone'. We have already learnt what a semitone is, but it is a good thing to check this up once again by asking the pupil to play whatever sharp is named. After this it is as well to describe flats as 'lowering a note one semitone', and ask the pupil to play the flats named. (Some teachers may, however, prefer to leave flats until later.) We must not forget, at this stage, that the pupil has not seen the written sign for sharp or flat. Here the manuscript book is used; they are written down to be copied, and an exercise set at the teacher's discretion. The scale of G is played correctly once again, as it is now understood why the seventh note had to be changed from F to F sharp.

Whenever a new scale is taught the order of tones and semitones should be revised, and the new sharp (or flat) discovered by the pupil himself. Each key signature should be written and copied, and the sharps and flats be learnt and repeated in their correct order.

The playing of scales should not be the only thing that is taught with relation to the key. Once the structure of the scale has been understood, there is no reason why very simple exercises in transposition should not be attempted. The pupil must now understand that most tunes are built on the notes of one of the scales. Pick out any simple tune you like, a nursery rhyme will do, or even 'God Save the Queen'. Play it (unharmonized) in several keys. Repeat it slowly in the key of C, numbering the notes from 1 to 8. For example, 'Baa Baa, Black Sheep' numbered would be 1 1 5 5 67865, 4 4 3 3 2 2 1. Write these numbers down and get the pupil to pick out the tune in the key of G, from the numbers (never mind the fingering and technique), remembering that 7 is F sharp. Quite a large number of children will do this completely successfully, and will be only too ready to try the same tune in other keys. I see no reason why this very musicianly side of the pupil's education should be considered so advanced that one never thinks of teaching it, apart from the theory lessons.

One more point that will explain a lot to the pupil later is the fact that many simple tunes, 'Little Bo Peep', for instance, are built on only the first five notes of the scale. This being so, the F sharp in the key of G is never played, and yet G is the 'home note' or Doh. This will solve the problem that perplexes so many young people: 'Why do they give a sharp in the key signature when there isn't one in the piece?' It must therefore be made clear that the signature represents a 'key' and tells us which is the key note, if we have learnt our keys properly.

It is now important that the pupil should be able to pick out the chord of each key he learns. There is no real difficulty in finding 1–3–5 of any scale, and the triad should be played in each key as it is taught. The more intelligent child will like to learn about inversions (the chord turned upside down), and another good test in finding a chord is to give such an example as this:

and ask the pupil to find what chord it is by playing it in its closest possible position.

Now we come to minor scales. If the scale, the key, and the piece are to be linked up in early lessons, then it will not be long before we need to know something about a minor key. Many First Grade pieces are written in the key of A minor, and their rather sad sound has an appeal for the imaginative child. Just as a small boy will like to know how the wheels go round in a piece of machinery, so an intelligent pupil will be interested to know how the 'sad sound' is produced, if we can find a simple enough explanation. I suppose the usual introduction to teaching a minor scale is to tell the pupil that every major key has a relative minor—I myself started in this way for years—but at last I have come to the conclusion that this is not the best approach to minor scales. If we are going to describe a character in a story, we do not proceed to talk about his or her relations first. We get to know the character, and the relations are introduced later.

So, then, the first thing to find out is what makes the piece sound sad. The teacher will tell the pupil that it is in what is called a minor key, and will play to the pupil the scale to which the piece belongs. (On the whole, it is easier to demonstrate the point with harmonic minors, but individuals may have their own ideas about this.) Supposing, then, we are to play the scale of A minor (harmonic). Get the pupil to turn away from the keyboard and ask him if he can tell which note is causing the sad sound. He may or may not be able to tell. If he is not successful, play only the first five notes and ask again: if still not successful, play the first five notes of minor followed by the first five of major. By now 80 per cent of your pupils will have discovered the sad third. Now we will look at the keyboard. What has happened to the third? It is only a semitone from the second, instead of a tone, as in the major scale. Now play the whole minor scale again, calling the semitones as they occur, and noticing that they occur between the second and third, fifth and sixth, seventh and eighth, and that there is always a wide interval between the sixth and seventh. To finish the first stage of the lessons on minor keys get the pupil again to turn away from the keyboard and recognize whether you are playing major or minor scales.

At the next lesson this little test can be repeated and a minor scale played by the pupil, who should, if possible, be learning a piece in the same key.

When this knowledge has been acquired and the playing of the scale mastered—possibly the following week—the pupil can be told of the relationship between major and minor.

Having stressed the importance of knowing that the relative minor may be found three semitones below the major, it is surprising to find how many pupils are completely at a loss when asked how they would find the relative major of a minor scale. Of course they must be able to answer this, and it is as well to turn the question upside down several times and ask: 'What is the relative minor of F major?' and then: 'What is the relative major of E minor', &c.

Now is the time to demonstrate in writing the similarity between the scales. Write a number of minor scales for the pupil to see. It does not matter whether he can play them or not; the point is to understand how they are formed from the major. In the case of A minor we put no key signature, as C major has none. We then start from A and write the eight notes of the octave. Next we tell the pupil that the seventh note has to be raised one semitone. To do this we must write something in front of it. What shall we write? With any luck the pupil will give the correct answer: that we should write a sharp in front of the G. Try not to give more answers yourself than are necessary; it is the things the child has discovered for himself that he remembers the best. After writing A minor, we will suggest that the pupil tells us what is the relative minor of G major (a reminder to count down three semitones may be necessary if the answer is not forthcoming). Now we will write the scale of E minor. This time we have to put a key signature of one sharp, because it is related to G major. The scale is then written up from E to E, and the pupil's attention drawn to the fact that there will be an F sharp in the scale, as it is in the key signature. But the scale is not complete yet: we still have to raise the seventh note. Again the answer should come from the pupil as to how to do this. All new minor scales that are taught should be written in this way, special care being taken to point out the fact that the seventh note is *not* always a sharp. For instance, in the keys of C and F minor, where the seventh note would be a flat according to the key signature, to raise that flat one semitone it must become a natural. (Later on will come the necessity for explaining in the same way the double sharp in G sharp minor.)

I have treated this matter rather exhaustively, because what is clear to the teacher is not always made clear enough to the pupil. Very often it is explained in the first instance, but never properly revised when each new minor key is taught.

As the pupil learns to find the major triad, so he will easily learn to find the minor triad. It is as well to point out that the major triad and its relative minor have two notes in common.

The next step is to determine whether a piece of music is in a major key or its relative minor. Try to impress on the pupil always to consider the possibility of the *two* keys when looking at a key signature. He should study the opening and final bars, which, except in unusual cases, will either be built on the notes of the triad or on a sequence of notes from the scale. The bass part is the best guide, and the keynote will almost invariably be found in the lowest part of the final chord. The raised seventh may appear in minor keys, but does not always do so, and cannot be taken as an infallible guide.

Once the pupil has progressed sufficiently far, the teacher should see that he always knows the key of any piece he may read or learn. He should be asked to name the key of several pieces shown to him, or, as a writing exercise, to fill in the keynote above certain pieces that the teacher sets.

Broken chords and arpeggios are treated in the same way as scales, and the pupil should be encouraged to work them out for himself with the knowledge that they are made up from the 1, 3, 5 of the scale.

Technically, broken chords require a good rotary action.

The accent falls on the first note of each group, and is made clear by adding extra exertion to the end finger joint plus a *little* added arm weight. The remaining notes are played lightly and easily, the fingers being 'guided' across the chord by the freedom of the arm (see Plate VI, Figs. 1–4). At the 'turn', the transference of accent from thumb to fifth finger (or vice versa) can be practised in the following way:

Fingering can be a difficulty, and to achieve correctness may need a good deal of firmness and perseverance on the part of the teacher. I find that the easiest way is to write the *fingering only* on a page of the note-book and get the pupil to follow it whilst playing in the different keys. Thus:

Right hand $\begin{cases} 1, 2, \circled{3}, 5. \\ 1, 2, \circled{4}, 5. \\ 1, 2, \circled{4}, 5. \\ 1, 2, \circled{3}, 5. \end{cases}$

Ascending

putting a ring round the essential third or fourth. It can also be pointed out that the third plays only when there are two notes between it and the top one (or the bottom one in the case of the left hand).

The change-over from one type of broken chord to another will be simplified if an exercise of this type is given:

Left Hand starts two octaves lower

Arpeggios are often found easier than broken chords, provided the pupil has a free lateral arm movement and a thumb which travels easily, as outlined in the scale technique. Here is a good preliminary exercise which can be played in several keys ascending and descending:

Two-octave arpeggios should not be played in groups of three. They can be practised in the following ways with varied accents:

Four octave arpeggios are played in groups of four. In slow practice the accent should be well defined. At speed it should, of course, not be too prominent, but just sufficient to give a rhythmical effect.

The arpeggios of the dominant and diminished seventh are not included in this book, but it can readily be seen that the same rules for practice, technique and varied accentuation can be applied to them.[1]

Chromatic scales have their place in the practice scheme of all young pianists. To teach them theoretically is not necessary in the early stages, the difference between harmonic chromatic and melodic chromatic will be understood later, or learned in the class lessons. These scales should be played as legato as possible (unless specified otherwise in an examination syllabus), and the thumb plays a great part in preserving this legato. There should be no 'bumps', as though the hand were 'falling' from black key to white. Mention of this thumb activity, and an exercise developing it, will be found on page 22.

With regard to the method of practising scales and arpeggios, the more that are known, the more methodical must be the practice. Lists, dividing them into groups, can be made, and during the lesson the teacher should ask for them in different ways, such as: 'Play the major scale which has a key signature of two sharps. Now play its relative minor. Play the triad in the key of F major. Now play it as an arpeggio,' and so on.

Though this book does not include suggestions for advanced students, it is a good thing to practise scales in a variety of ways, especially when the pupil reaches Grade V Associated Board (or an equivalent Grade at which all major and minor keys must be known). Much will be gained in finger control if different rhythms are tried out, such as ♩♪♩♪ or (an especially good one for three-octave scales) ♪♪♩♪♪♩ Both scales and arpeggios can be played legato or staccato, and with different gradations of tone. Practice in different tonal balance between the hands (where one hand plays

---

[1] Further examples for scale and arpeggio practice appear in *Freedom Technique* by Joan Last (O.U.P. – 3 books).

louder than the other) can be given, and this will help the pupil with contrapuntal music and part playing.

Another variety of practice, which is found less easy, is to commence the scale on some other note than the keynote.

The main thing is for the student to get a 'key sense,' and not practise scales and arpeggios blindly with the idea that they are something extremely dull which has to be got through before the more interesting part is attempted. Whilst one cannot predict that they will ever achieve popularity, they can at least be presented in as interesting a way as possible, and their relationship to familiar tunes, or their occurrence in pieces, pointed out. In this way the pupil will learn to practise them intelligently, and will see the reason for the necessity to learn them if he is to become a pianist who is also a musician.

AURAL WORK

AURAL training is an essential part of the piano lesson in the early stages, though it is often not possible to spend very long over it. There always seems so much to be done in such a short time. This lack of time, this sense of rush, is part of the price we have to pay for living in an enlightened age. Not only do the pupils have too many other things to do to give more time to music, but the teachers are forced to charge too much for their time to enable many parents to afford long lessons. It seems so sad, now that the ideas on music teaching are advancing almost daily, that one scarcely has time to put one's ideals into practice. However, there is one great advantage in modern education which helps the music teacher enormously, and that is the inclusion of aural training classes in the curriculum of nearly all schools.

The examiners who sit in judgement on the ordinary piano pupil, and who pronounce the standard of aural tests throughout the country to be deplorable (and they are quite right), probably have no idea that examination preparation may consist of one half-hour lesson per week, in which the teacher has to prepare the pupil in scales, arpeggios, pieces, sight-reading, *and* aural tests. These tests cannot be done in a few minutes a week unless the pupil has a natural ear, and I have found that a really poor ear cannot be improved more than about 10 per cent throughout the course of one term, possibly not even that if there are no aural training classes in the child's school. We are all familiar with the aural tests which are set, in a gradually rising spiral of difficulty, throughout the Examination Grades. I often think that for those who find them hard, it is because they have never been taught to LISTEN to music, but only to HEAR it. This listening faculty can be developed in other ways that are less exacting for the pupil with a poor ear, and more encouraging and interesting to all.

The first thing, then, which a pianist should learn is to LISTEN, and yet, strangely enough, many quite advanced pianists never appear to listen to *themselves*. They think they do, of course, but their critical faculty has not been developed, and they have not learnt to get more than a surface impression of what they are doing.

The pupil need not have advanced very far before he realizes that music has what might be described as 'Shape'. By listening to simple phrases played by the teacher, or by playing them himself, he will discover that a mere handful of notes can be played in a number of different ways. The following will illustrate the point:

a) To be played by the teacher with as level a tone as possible

b) Now we will put in some 'shape'

The pupil should be asked which he prefers, and be invited to make suggestions. New phrases should be introduced and experimented with, all suggestions, if possible, now coming from the pupil.

Here are some typical melodies which would be useful for these tests. Not only could expression marks be added. Staccato, legato, accents, and slurs should be illustrated, to show how the character of the music can be varied:

Now we will go a step further in developing this critical faculty. Let the teacher and pupil change places. Those who have taken a Teacher's Diploma may remember the examiner seating himself at the keyboard and making deliberate mistakes for their detection. Why not give the pupil the same kind of test in miniature? Not only should mistakes in notes and time be given, but the pupil should listen for faulty tone, missed rests, time hurried or dragged, staccato omitted, tied notes missed, expression not observed, and so on. It is surprising how critical a young child can be, and I have often been pulled up for 'mistakes' which I did not know I was making!

Later a piece might be simply analysed, and questions asked as to time, key, length of phrases, and so on, according to the grade of the pupil. It will be evident that other questions may lead from the first, and in this way the pupil learns something of the construction of the piece.

The harmonic side is not so easy, and cannot be gone into in much detail, unless a complete digression from the piano lesson takes place. However, the pupil can recognize when the piece 'comes home' to the keynote, and which bars are built on the scale, or chord. It is difficult to draw the line when writing a book which relates mainly to *playing* the piano, but a certain amount of understanding as to how the composer works develops the interpretative faculty as no amount of technical practice will, and the musical child will particularly enjoy these forms of musical exploration.

If the listening faculty is developed in the way I have just outlined, it should be easier to bring it to bear on the ordinary aural tests with which we are familiar. For these there have been excellent books written, and it is not within the scope of this book to do more than suggest ways of teaching a few of those that are to be found in the Grades 1 to 5.

Time and rhythm tests appear to present less difficulty for the average pupil than pitch tests. The clapping of time patterns is usually quite well done, so long as the test is short enough to be retained in the memory. Where the longer patterns are required and the memory is not able to retain them, it is useless to play them over and over again: the pupil simply gets into a kind of mental fog, and loses all sense of pulse and rhythm. This difficulty can be tackled in two parts. First of all, shorter tests must be given, and an effort made to build up the length gradually. Secondly, a long test can be played and the pupil told to listen only to the pulse and determine the *time*. On the second listening he tries to get the beginning of the pattern, improvising the rest of it and trying to make sure it is of the same length and in the correct time. The answer may not be completely correct, but it is at least nearer the mark! The main thing is to *keep the rhythm going*, and not to stop and think. An answer of this kind would gain higher marks at an examination than one that was completely vague and rhythmless.

It will be found that some children have remarkably little

control over the action of clapping, and can manage much better if they are allowed to tap the time-values on a table or the lid of the piano. These children should be shown how they can make one hand into a table, or imagine that it is a drum or tambourine, whilst the other taps out the pattern on it. The hand that does the tapping should have an easy relaxed action, which also helps towards a staccato action on the piano (see Plate VII, Figs. 1 and 2, facing p. 100).

Occasionally one will come across the child whose rhythmical sense is really weak. The first problem here will be to get him to clap or tap the *pulse* whilst music is being played in a steady time. Examples in compound time are the best to begin with, and must, of course, be played very rhythmically, with the beats well accented. When the child can keep time with the music he should be told to listen for a change in speed, either faster or slower, and to keep with the music all the time. When this is accomplished we demonstrate the difference between crotchets and quavers or 'walking and running notes' and play (for example) four bars of each for the child to follow and clap.

In this way the rhythmic sense is gradually developed, and it will be seen how the training can be continued on these lines over a period of time.

The recognition of the time (2/4, 3/4 or 4/4, &c) is usually done correctly after a little practice. *At first* the teacher should put a very strong accent on the first beat of the bar. The pupil should only feel the *first* beat at this stage, and could just tap his hand on his leg, or clap the first beat. Next he learns to make a downward movement on the strong beat, and finally to fill in the remaining beats with the appropriate movements. These movements are known as: two beats = down, up; three beats = down, right, up; four beats = down, left, right, up (not down, *right*, left, up). Provided they are correctly done, marks in examinations are not lost for stiff or angular movements; at the same time, beating time can be much more rhythmically done if these angular movements are avoided. For two beats, instead of drawing an imaginary straight line up and down, a slight curve will bring more rhythmic swing into the beat, and the same applies to three and four time. Diagrams such as the following can be drawn on a large piece of cardboard for the pupil to follow. The lines should be about 18 inches long, and the bottom of the down movement should not be taken below waist level:

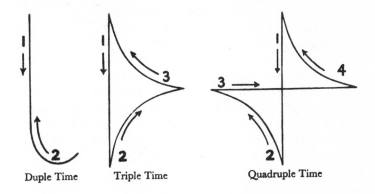

Duple Time   Triple Time   Quadruple Time

Pitch tests present difficulty in a greater number of cases than do rhythmic tests. In young children the rhythmic sense develops sooner than the pitch sense, and the fact that a child does not sing in tune at the age of seven or eight does not mean that he has no ear. With many it is that they cannot yet 'place' the voice exactly where they wish. These children are commonly called 'growlers' in the singing class, and to some of them this stigma remains and singing becomes a thing they just cannot face up to.

I have no specialist's knowledge of voice-training, and can only offer a few suggestions which may be of use. The child who will never sing, and is what is called 'tone deaf', is in a very small minority indeed, and for this minority there is, of course, nothing to be done. We are concerned here with those who cannot *yet* sing in tune, but who will do so before long.

The first thing is for them to realize that it is only a matter of practice. They will respond better if given plenty of 'listening' tests. First the teacher can play a note and attempt to sing it herself, sometimes correctly, and sometimes incorrectly, for the pupil to detect the difference. Or the child can play a note on the piano while the teacher shuts her eyes, and then tries to find the correct note (here again making mistakes for the pupil to detect). Now the teacher plays a note and the pupil finds it on the piano. Perhaps he is quite wrong, and unable to get near the mark. The teacher will say: 'Was that too low or too high? Now listen again, and I will sing the note while you find it.' The note is found at last; and the next step is for the pupil to sing *any note he likes* for the teacher to find. A so-called 'growler' may sing a very low note, and, when it has been found, it can be pointed out to him that of course he can sing, but he happens to have rather a low voice, and must now try and gradually learn to go up a little higher. So we start on this low note and see if we can build up a scale from it, in the same way as we play a scale on the piano.

All this may take a lot of time and patience, but it is quite amazing in some cases to notice the gradual enlarging of the range of notes reached by the child. I know that one often feels there simply isn't time for this sort of thing; but there are moments when we have to put first things first and decide which is more important, a few new bars of a piece, or something which, when achieved, will stay with the child throughout his musical career.

Finally we come to the singing of melodies. It is a good plan to start with well-known ones if the sense of pitch has been weak. When new ones are given they should, at first, be very short. Here again the teacher might invite the pupil to listen and correct any mistakes she makes in singing a short melody previously played.

A few melodies are given here which might serve as a starting point from which to build:

These tests should, of course, be played at whatever pitch best suits the child's voice. Only very simple ones have been given because I am dealing with the child who finds singing tests difficult, not the one who does not need this kind of help.

When the singing of a melody can be easily managed, the time has come to try to name the notes after the tonic has been given. A real knowledge of the key and scale as outlined in a previous chapter will be a tremendous help in this test. I suggest that the notes of the chord 1, 3, 5 are revised and named in two or three keys. The keys of C, G, and F would be best for a start. A little melody such as 1, 3, 5, 5, 1 is played, and the pupil identifies the notes in the key of C, and then himself plays the melody in the keys of G and F. This is just a beginning, and in a subsequent test he names the notes by heart instead of playing them. When the notes of the chord can be easily recognized and named, the second is added, and new melodies given in which it is included— e.g. 1, 3, 5, 5, 3, 2, 1. Again we wait until the pupil can recognize these four degrees of the scale before taking another step. This time the fourth is added, later the octave, and finally the sixth and seventh.

Very briefly I have outlined a process that may perhaps take a year or more, but all these things are much easier for the pupil if they are built up gradually. In this case it is most important to know really well the keys in which the intervals are likely to be given. Some pupils find that it is a help to look at the keyboard whilst giving the answers, and this could be done at first, but they must eventually learn to do without this help. Musical dictation, if given in progressive stages, is a great help, and it is well worth while to give an occasional dictation to be written in the place of the oral answer.

We now come to recognizing and singing the higher or lower of two notes played simultaneously on the piano. For the pupil who can imitate a melody there is seldom any difficulty in hearing the higher, but the lower often causes quite a lot of trouble. At first the teacher should split the chord, playing the higher note first and putting more emphasis on the lower note. When this has been recognized and correctly sung, a sequence similar to the following should be played, and it will probably be found that the pupil can follow the lower line of melody quite easily once his ear has, as it were, been attuned to it :

If, on the other hand, a two-part chord is played at another pitch, the pupil may have renewed difficulty in hearing the lower note, and the whole process will have to be repeated. By this means the pupil gradually learns to separate the two sounds in his mind, though it may be some considerable time before he gives a correct answer in the first instance.

Next we add a third note, and here again the pupil will have to be gradually worked up to hearing the three sounds. The chords again should be split, so that the separate sounds become clearer. On the whole, it is easier to sing the sounds from top to bottom, but, of course, both ways must be practised. When it comes to recognizing triads in their different positions, it is definitely easier for the pupil if taught to sing (at first audibly, but later mentally) from the top downwards. He then has to decide in his mind whether the lowest note was the root, third, or fifth of the chord. If the root, it has a final sound; if it is not the root, then the pupil continues to sing down the arpeggio until he feels that the root is reached. If he needs to add one further note downwards to complete the chord, then it was a first inversion with the third at the bottom; if two notes, then it was a second inversion with the fifth at the bottom.

These singing tests are so bound up with the recognizing and naming of intervals that they should be taught side by side with them, beginning from the time when the pupil can sing the two notes of an interval.

The octave is usually easy to recognize, especially if played alternately with its unison. From this point I have found it surprisingly successful to introduce intervals in pairs and describe them according to their 'character'. Thus we get 2nds and 7ths—ugly intervals. 3rd and 6ths—'kind intervals'. 4ths and 5ths—'bare intervals'. The pupil first recognizes the order in which such pairs are played, being asked, for example: 'Is this pair a 3rd and 6th or a 6th and 3rd?' The hardest pair to separate is the 4th and 5th and here we might try 'singing up', at first audibly *but not if for an examination*. The pupil has to learn to 'sing mentally'. Let the pupil learn that one interval is an *Inversion* of its 'partner' and play them himself. From this beginning single isolated intervals seem easier. The two notes can be separated at first and may even be related to the opening of familiar tunes. Eventually, of course, the two notes should be played together.

There is no doubt that aural perception is largely a matter of natural ability, and the advantage of having a good ear is very great in examinations. I hope that one day all examining bodies will combine with aural work questions on tempo, key, phrasing, expression, and so forth, according to the Grade, using prepared and unprepared examples. The conscientious and hard-working candidate who is weak at ear tests could then furnish some proof, apart from keyboard work, of general musical intelligence.

TIME AND RHYTHM

THE difference between time and rhythm is often not clearly understood, and this is largely due to the number of different meanings that are applied to the word 'rhythm'.

One can ask a pupil to clap a rhythm or rhythmic pattern, and the correct response should be an exact imitation of certain time values; but if one says that a person has a good sense of rhythm, one implies something more than the ability to clap or play exactly in time. It is possible for two people to clap the values of a certain phrase correctly, and yet for one to do so more rhythmically than the other. If the same phrase were played on a musical instrument, the difference between these two would be even more noticeable. Melody relies upon rhythm to make it come alive, and the mere playing of correct time values cannot do that.

Rhythm, in its true sense, includes the pulse and swing of the music: its natural accent, which leads to phrasing, tonal variety, climax, and so on. It would be better if the word rhythm were never used as meaning a time-pattern, for it is here that the confusion arises.

A sense of rhythm is born in nearly everyone to a greater or lesser degree. Far fewer people in the world are devoid of a rhythmic sense than are lacking in a sense of pitch. Millions of people who have never studied music will respond to the rhythm of a dance tune, or will instinctively walk along the road in time with the music of a military band. This sense is certainly developed more strongly and in a more subtle way in the musician, but it is not, in essence, a thing that has to be *taught*.

Time values, on the other hand, have to be taught from the beginning. They are the arithmetic of music.

In this chapter I am going to talk about Time first, because it has to be *taught*, whilst Rhythm is *developed*.

The knowledge of time values and time signatures is built up stage by stage, and, as in note-reading, the teaching should be detailed, thorough, and unhurried. See that the pupil really *understands* each stage before going on to the next. By the end of the first term the average child should certainly be able to read and name semibreves, minims, and crotchets, and understand the meaning of 2/4 and 4/4 time. He will also probably have learnt about dotted minims, quavers, and 3/4 time. The rests corresponding to each note should be taught as the pupil progresses. It is likely that tied notes, in a simple form, will have been included, such as those that come at the end of a phrase. For example:

The pupil with good natural rhythm will, however, be able to clap by imitation patterns which include many more time values than those he can read. There is no need for him to be able to *name* them all; that will be taught gradually. The names are, in any case, less important than the arithmetical side. The immediate reaction to this, ♩, should be 'two beats' rather than 'a minim'. Though music is spoken of as an 'international language', in that the written page conveys the same *sound* to students of all countries, the word 'minim' is by no means 'international'.[1] Possibly the simplest method of naming time values is that used in America (see table on page 68).

During the first few weeks the reading of notes and time cannot be combined with very much success. The pupil is far too busy 'finding the note' to have the further complication of playing in time. For this reason I have given semibreves

[1] Students and teachers should study the terminology of the various countries. These can be found in *The Oxford Companion to Music*, Percy Scholes (O.U.P.).

to be read at the first lesson on page 14. The reading
practice at this stage needs to be divided into two parts. The
first part is the reading of notes, and the second part is the
reading of time (by clapping, or beating a percussion instrument). These two stages gradually merge into one as the
pupil progresses. The idea could be carried out something
on these lines:

First Stage.   Note reading in semibreves.
               Time reading of crotchets and minims.
Second Stage. Note reading—minims added.
               Time reading—semibreves added.
Third Stage.   Note reading—semibreve rests added.
               Time reading—quavers added.
Fourth Stage. Note reading—minim rests added.
               Time reading—as before.
Fifth Stage.   Note reading—crotchets added, and their rests.
               Time reading—as before.

The pupil has now combined the reading of time and notes
on a five-note compass to include semibreves, minims,
crotchets, and their rests.

Quavers will be included in the note reading as soon as
the pupil can recognize notes at a glance. Occasionally one
hears a distortion of groups of quavers, such as ♩ ♫ ♩ ♩
in place of ♩ ♫ ♩ ♩ The pupil who does this is probably
perfectly capable of clapping quavers by imitation, but their
first appearance on the printed page is misleading. Seeing
the two quavers, he thinks: 'Two quick ones and then back to
slow ones'. He has not realized that the quick movement does
not finish until the next crotchet is reached, and so he 'iso-
lates' the quavers. This trouble can soon be overcome if the
pupil claps an even flow of quavers, counting: 'One-and, two-
and, three-and, four-and' continuously, whilst the teacher
plays the pattern in question. This is followed by the teacher
clapping the quavers whilst the pupil plays the pattern.
Later new patterns are introduced which include quavers
in different groupings.

Some teachers prefer to give one count for each quaver, particularly when the music is in 2/4 time, or where semi-quavers are included. The one difficulty here is that the pupil is apt to get confused, for he will have to count two for a crotchet and four for a minim. However, if satisfactory results can be got that way, it is as good as any other. The French time names are another way of teaching time values, though, on the whole, these seem to lend themselves better to class work, or to piano lessons of the really small pupils, who are learning mainly by rote.

We must remember, in the early stages, that if a pupil reads out of time it does not necessarily mean that he does not understand the time values, or that his rhythmic sense is weak. I sometimes feel that we do expect rather a lot from our beginners. We should remind ourselves that to play *one note* they must: Look at the written page and mentally translate the sign they see into a letter of the alphabet; find the note on the keyboard which represents that letter of the alphabet; decide with which finger to strike the key; perform the correct movements of hand and arm to strike the key clearly and decisively. And when they have done all this successfully, the unreasonable teacher exclaims: 'Why can't you play in time'! Why indeed?

Now we come to the dotted crotchet. This is often found difficult. The first question is: 'What effect does a dot have on the note after which it is placed?' It is better if this is explained when the dotted minim is learnt, though it is quite easy just to say that the dot adds one more beat on to the minim. However, this simple explanation may add confusion over other dotted notes. It is one of those things that cannot be wrapped up like the chocolate-coated pill. Here again I would call it the arithmetic of music, and it must be taught as such. The average child likes to *understand* what he is doing, and there is nothing more satisfying than the moment when the teacher and pupil both realize that the lesson *has* been understood.

So, at the beginning of a lesson (not when there are only five minutes left) the teacher will explain the dot. To say: 'A dot makes the note half as long again', will cause some confusion in the mind of the child, and an explanation that is more easily understood is: 'The dot is worth half the note after which it is placed'. We then work out the following with pencil and paper, the answers coming whenever possible from the pupil:

Semibreve = 4 beats.	Its dot = 2 beats.	𝅝· = 4 + 2. 6 beats.
Minim = 2 beats.	Its dot = 1 beat.	𝅗𝅥· = 2 + 1. 3 beats.
Crotchet = 1 beat.	Its dot = ½ beat.	𝅘𝅥· = 1 + ½. 1½ beats.

(Dotted quavers, &c., are left for a later lesson.)

The knowledge that the dotted crotchet is worth one and a half does not, however, mean that the pupil has learnt to play it correctly. The easiest way for the pupil to learn to play the dotted crotchet is to approach it in this way:

Teacher: 'We have just found out that the dot after a crotchet is worth half the crotchet. Can you tell me what note value is worth half a crotchet?' *Answer*: 'A quaver.' *Teacher*: 'So you are really going to hold the note down for one quaver longer.' The teacher then writes:

𝅘𝅥 𝅘𝅥𝅮𝅘𝅥𝅮 𝅘𝅥

Teacher: 'Can you tell me what the curved line between the crotchet and first quaver means?' *Answer*: 'It is a tie.' *Teacher*: 'Now I will put my pencil through the second note to remind you that you only "think it"; you do not actually play it:

𝅘𝅥 𝅘𝅥𝅮𝅘𝅥𝅮 𝅘𝅥

First of all we will take it as a clapping exercise. I am going to write the bar again without the tie. Will you clap and count.'

One (and) two-and, three (and)

𝅘𝅥   𝅘𝅥𝅮𝅘𝅥𝅮   𝅘𝅥

'That is quite easy. Now clap it two or three times. Now we will clap the two versions running, counting in the same way.'

♩ ♫ ♩ | ♩ ♫ ♩

If the pupil finds this difficult, the teacher should play the straightforward version on the piano whilst the pupil claps the tied note version to fit in, thus:

Teacher ♩ ♫ ♩

Pupil ♩ ♫ ♩

The teacher then writes these two lines, reminding the pupil that, as a dot is worth a quaver, there is no difference between the first and second lines:

1. ♩ ♫ ♩ | ♩ ♫ ♩

2. ♩ · ♪ ♩ | ♩ · ♪ ♩

One (and two) and three

This is followed by various clapping exercises to include the dotted crotchet, which should be revised at subsequent lessons, e.g.:

4/4 ♩ ♫ ♩ ♩ | ♩. ♪ ♩ ♩ | ♩ ♩ ♩. ♪ | 𝅝 ‖

Semiquavers are quite easy to play in time provided the fingers are nimble enough. As he becomes more advanced, the pupil should learn to recognize at a glance the groups of different time values that make up a crotchet. Progressively they might be taught in this order:

One crotchet equals } each of these groups

♫ ♬ ♫♬ ♬♫ ♩.♬

The dotted quaver will be explained in a way similar to the dotted crotchet, but it is less easy to play in accurate time. Assuming that it is followed by a semiquaver, many pianists substitute this which, of course, is quite wrong. If they do so, the teacher should first write a group of four semiquavers, with the dotted quaver and semiquaver over the top.

It will be seen that the pianist should play on the first and fourth of a group of four. Next the teacher writes a group of three semiquavers, and shows, by musical illustration, that the pupil was in fact playing on the first and third of a group of three.

Time signatures never need be difficult to understand if the teacher makes a diagram for the pupil which explains the meaning of the bottom figure. In this the semibreve is called a whole note, and is subdivided as follows:

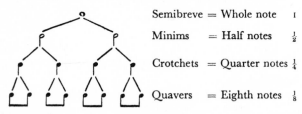

Semibreve	= Whole note	1
Minims	= Half notes	$\frac{1}{2}$
Crotchets	= Quarter notes	$\frac{1}{4}$
Quavers	= Eighth notes	$\frac{1}{8}$

The top figure, of course, denotes 'how many'. Exercises are set to make quite sure the pupil has grasped this lesson. The pupil supplies the answer to such as the following $2/4 = ?$, $3/8 = ?$, $4/2 = ?$, and so on.

I am not suggesting that a pupil will need to understand every figure found in simple time before he is introduced to compound time, but for the sake of clarity it has been easier to deal in some detail with simple time first.

I am going to assume that 6/8 is the first compound time

that is learnt, but the same method of teaching will apply to all compound times.

When the pupil first meets 6/8 time, the teacher will ask 'What does 6/8 mean?' If the pupil has understood the table which I have just given he will answer: 'Six quavers in a bar.' To begin with, this is quite correct. The six quavers in compound time are then written by the teacher thus:

$$\frac{6}{8} \; \text{♪♪♪ ♪♪♪}$$

and she points out to the pupil that they are grouped in threes. She then plays an even flow of quavers with a clearly defined accent at the beginning of each group to demonstrate how this will sound. The next question is: 'How many quavers are there in 3/4 time?' Again it is six, and the teacher here writes and plays an even flow of quavers in 3/4 time, accenting the 3 beats in a bar. The pupil will see that it is the *grouping* that makes the difference, and should be able to recognize alternate sets of 3/4 or 6/8 quavers played to him. Now the question comes: 'If there are two strong beats in 6/8 time, what is each of these beats worth?' This is a bit of a problem for the pupil, and the teacher will probably need to remind him that each beat is worth 3 quavers and to think of something that is worth 3 quavers. Here again the answer is slow in coming, until the pupil is reminded that it is to be a dotted note. At last we get the answer, 'A dotted crotchet', and the pupil will see that the two strong beats in 6/8 time are dotted crotchets, and that, because the beats are *dotted* notes, it is called *compound time*. It is a good thing to follow this with examples of time patterns in 9/8 and 12/8, though these two time signatures are less common than 6/8. Later on, other compound times will be worked out by pupil and teacher in much the same way.

As in simple time we teach the pupil to recognize the groups of notes that make up a crotchet, so in 6/8 time the pupil learns to know the groups which make up a dotted crotchet. At first this one is most important : ♩ ♪, and patterns should be given for clapping in which it is frequently included. When first reading 6/8 rhythms it may be necessary to count the six quavers. It is a good thing to repeat the same time pattern several times until the pupil can clap it counting two. The natural swing of compound time cannot be really felt whilst the subdivisions of the beat are being counted.

By now the pupil can no longer be called a beginner, and will need to be able to cope with such things as triplets and (a little later still) 'two against three' or 'cross time'. Let us take triplets first. Often these are not well played. Over and over again on public occasions, such as music festivals or concerts given by young people, I have heard a group of triplets played thus:

There is a similarity between this distortion and that of the group of two quavers which are played thus: ♫. ♩ The cause is very much the same. The triplet speed must not be suddenly halted at the last of the three quavers, but must run on to the crotchet which follows. The pupil should be able to cure this using the words:

One-and-a-Two

Incidentally, he may come across duplet quavers in compound time, and if they cause difficulty they can be played correctly against a semiquaver rhythm (played or clapped by the teacher).

These two problems lead us naturally to 'two against three'. This can be taught in the following way: The teacher first writes a group of six notes (quavers will illustrate this the most clearly for a start). Assuming that the right hand is to play the triplet and the left hand the duplet, she will divide the group into three equal parts, writing a Capital 'R' (for 'right hand') over the first note of each part. She will then divide the group into two equal parts, writing 'L' (for 'left hand') under the first note of each part:

Next the teacher plays on the piano an even flow of six quavers whilst the pupil claps first those taken by the right hand and then those taken by the left hand. This is followed by the teacher and pupil *counting* out loud whilst the teacher takes one part and the pupil the other. It will now clearly be heard that the combined clapping makes this rhythm:

It is pointed out that on the first beat of each group both teacher and pupil clapped together, so that the final result is:

At a quicker speed the rhythm might equally well be written as this:

which is the rhythm formed by 'Two against three' in quavers.

An easy melody and accompaniment is devised for practice such as:

etc.

At first it is played very slowly, but the speed must be gradually increased. It follows that, once this has been successfully done, the pupil must learn to play the three in the left hand and two in the right.

etc.

'Three against four' can be worked out in the same way, starting from a basis of twelve quavers, thus:

$$\overset{\text{R}}{}\quad\overset{\text{R}}{}\quad\overset{\text{R}}{}\quad\overset{\text{R}}{}$$

Perhaps before leaving the subject of time I should mention 'syncopation', which is the displacement of the natural accent. It is not altogether a case of arithmetic, though it is not usually found difficult so long as there is a steady pulse maintained in one hand. Where that pulse is not played, and has only to be *felt*, we are getting near to the place where time and rhythm meet. A pupil who works the matter out by arithmetic, but has a poor sense of rhythm, will be able to count and play at a *slow* speed, and will also be able to clap the rhythm whilst the teacher plays an even flow of quavers. But where the rhythmic sense is really weak, no amount of arithmetic will enable the pupil to give a satisfactory performance of the following:

From **Serenade of the Doll**   **Debussy**

To the unrhythmical pupil the teacher will have to say: 'Leave it for the present, and as you continue your musical studies your rhythmic sense will develop more strongly and you will be able to "feel" the syncopated rhythm. It cannot be done by *counting*.'

How, then, can rhythm be developed? It is a case of awakening rhythmic perception to the highest limit of each individual.

First of all we must remember that the word 'rhythm' does not apply only to music. The whole manifestation of life and nature is built on rhythm: an orderly sequence of events, night and day, the phases of the moon, the seasons, the growth of plants, and so on. This sense of rhythm is brought to bear in all the arts, and even in manual occupation. The student of drawing learns the rules of perspective, but without a natural sense of rhythm he cannot make his drawings live. The dancer learns the technique of the dance, but without rhythm of movement cannot convey the beauty of the dance to others. The athlete must learn the rhythmic co-ordination of his muscles if he is to succeed. The actor must learn to speak and move in a way that gives a rhythmic flow to the words and harmonizes with others on the stage. Even the manual worker finds his work less tiring if he moves in a rhythmical way.

However, we cannot apply these ideas to the young child struggling to understand the first laws of rhythm, as in music: for here we have to bring the meaning of rhythm down to something much more tangible which can be demonstrated and understood by the young mind.

One fact, however, can be made clear and that is the difference of tonal *amount* needed between notes of long or short duration. The rule could be 'the quicker the note the lighter the arm'. To illustrate I quote some rhythmic patterns which, if the prefaced instruction is followed, will move from 'arithmetic to rhythm'.

1.　Soften the crotchets.
2.　Soften the quavers.
3.　Soften the semiquavers.

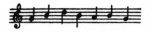

(a)
(b)
(c)

The teacher can play such groups with and without the softened notes and the pupil asked to comment. Having commented he listens carefully to give a reason for preference (only rarely does a child fail to do this. I have mentioned listening and criticizing in the chapter on aural work and this sense of discovery is always valuable to the pupil.

Further criticism can be invited where the time signature is not clearly indicated in performance. Here a tune is played in three different ways. The teacher comments as she plays.

'I am going to play a little tune in rather a dull way':

'Now I will make it more interesting':

'You notice I played some notes louder than others; we call these accents. Will you clap the accents?' (Teacher repeats last performance.) 'Now count two as you clap.' (Pupil claps, counting two.)

'Now I will play exactly the same notes in another way':

'What is the difference? The accents are on different notes. This time clap the accents, and see what the counts are.'

It is likely that the pupil will realize that you are now playing the tune in three time.

The lesson to be learnt from this is not so much that the pupil should *recognize* the time (as in aural tests), but that he should realize that the pianist conveys the time of a piece to the listener by the *way* in which he plays the music. The tests which the teacher has just played, being extremely simple, should now be played by the pupil. It is a good plan for the pupil to try to convey to the teacher which one he is playing by his performance of it.

It is very probable that the pupil, in his efforts to make the time clear, will overdo the accents, and the next step is to learn to control the tone in such a way that the natural accent does not become monotonous. The principle is applied to the tunes or pieces which the pupil is learning, and the difference between the accent in two such contrasted pieces as a March and a Lullaby can be pointed out.

Where the piece does not begin on the first beat of the bar, it is very important that the pupil should realize that the anacrusis is *leading* to the first beat and that there should be no accent until the first beat is reached. There is often a tendency for the first notes to be isolated from the first beat; the pupil seems to find it difficult to get going in the rhythm at which he intends to continue. Often these first few notes are played at a different speed or with a different type of tone from that which follows. The pupil should learn to anticipate the whole of the first phrase in his mind and feel the 'pull' towards the first accented note. This 'pull' is the natural forward impulse which is an expression of rhythm and harmony combined. A pianist who has no feeling for this forward impulse cannot convey it to his audience, and to them it is like listening to a conversation which has neither point nor meaning, though the words may appear to make sense.

To take a very simple example. Supposing a pianist were to play this unfinished phrase:

There are very few people, whether they have studied music or not, who would not be surprised that nothing followed the last note.

This sense of expectancy is a manifestation of the ear's tendency to 'listen ahead', and this is what all musicians do. Here it is the unresolved harmony which leaves the ear unsatisfied. An unbalanced or unfinished rhythmic sequence can have exactly the same effect:

The pupil must learn to carry the impulse of each figure or phrase to its conclusion. This means, of course, that the piece must be well known, for uncertainty and stumbling over notes break the rhythmic impulse at once. Practising should be directed to this end. Let the pupil take a figure and practise it several times, with his mind and fingers directed towards the last note:

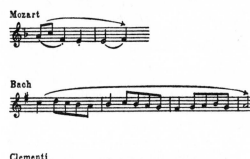

In the following the impulse moves to the G in the last bar, with the final quavers fading slightly:

Where the melody passes from one hand to the other, the continuity must not be broken:

An appreciation of rhythm and of bar lengths leads almost imperceptibly to that of phrasing and of the structure of a very simple piece. It is more easily understood by the pupil if phrasing is at first likened to the lines of a poem, and the first lessons on phrase lengths should be given with a rhyme set to music. This could be followed at the next lesson with a performance by the teacher of a very simple piece. The little Mozart Minuet in F or one of the Bach Anna Magdalena set would do very well. This type of lesson, as mentioned in an earlier part of the book, is very successful if given in class. I have found that a class of children aged from seven to eleven take great delight in listening to, and analysing, the rhythmic structure of a short piece.

The teacher first plays the piece through, and the child (by quietly clapping on the first beat of the bar) decides what time it is in. The teacher then repeats to the end of the first section and asks the pupil how many phrases were in this section. Next it is decided how many bars there are in each phrase. It is best to use, for these early lessons, pieces which have phrases of equal lengths, so that the pupil can hear that in music, as in poetry, the rhythm flows more easily if the phrases are balanced. (The question of unequal phrase lengths by augmentation, diminution &c., comes very much later.) The second section is divided up in the same way, and the lesson might even be extended to the comparison of examples of binary and ternary form. But this is more likely to be possible if the lesson is taken in class, as here the main point is to teach the pupil to indicate, by his *own* performance, the phrase-lengths of a piece.

The ability to do this depends on how far the interpretative faculty is developed. The art of interpretation as applied to the young pianist is discussed later in the book, where there will be found a great deal more about rhythm in piano-playing.

SIGHT-READING

THE natural ability to read does vary most considerably. A few there are who seem to be blessed with the faculty to read almost before they are taught the notes. How lucky they are! But these fortunate few are in a very small minority, and we teachers have, primarily, to consider those who do not find it so easy. For them sight-reading requires PRACTICE, MORE PRACTICE, and STILL MORE PRACTICE. No teaching can produce results without it. From the first lesson, when the pupil can read only two or three notes, to the time when a real interpretation is given, the rule should be: 'Read something new every day'. At first it may be four bars long and on single notes, but if this is done from the beginning a lot of trouble and struggle will be avoided later on.

It seems difficult to impress this on most young pupils. A piece can be learnt in a comparatively short time, and played with some satisfaction, but the few notes that they can read do not give them the same feeling of attainment. One can say to a child: 'If you do not practise your sight-reading you will regret it later on'. But it will have much the same effect as saying: 'If you do not eat your rice-pudding you will not grow big and strong'. Neither the reading nor the rice-pudding become any more popular as a result. Somehow or other we have to coax the pupil along until sight-reading does become a pleasure.

During the first term the pupil builds up, step by step, his knowledge of notation and time values. This should not be hurried; each step should be perfected before another one is taken. A slow child may take several weeks to learn to recognize and read the few notes which I suggested in the first lesson. To avoid monotony they should, in this case, be presented in a number of different ways. Time values can be varied, as the average child will learn a new time value more easily than new notes. Let us assume, then, that for six consecutive lessons we get no farther than three notes in each hand. For the first lesson they can be taught in the straightforward way given earlier in the book. In the second lesson the teacher can write a time signature, 4/4, and explain that this means four beats in a bar (we cannot use the word crotchets yet, because the crotchet has not been learnt). She will then insert the bar lines, and the reading lesson proceeds much as before. In the third lesson the pupil is still uncertain over the notes, but should not be allowed to feel that he is stupid. Instead something new is taught—minims. These are worth two beats, and the pupil will be shown an unbarred sequence of minims, and be asked to insert the bar lines. The reading then proceeds, again on the *same notes*, but with minim beats. At the fourth lesson the time is varied, by the admixture of minims and semibreves, and in the fifth the semibreve rest is taught. In the sixth lesson a little tune is given which passes from one hand to another.

Readers of this book may not have had a pupil whose perception is as slow as this, but they will be very lucky if one does not come their way before long. It means, of course, that the exercises for reading will have to be written in a manuscript book, as no known book of sight-reading proceeds quite as slowly as this.

The manuscript book is also used for the pupil to write names under the given notes, or add bar lines to unbarred rhythmic patterns, fill in rests, and so on, as each stage is reached.

This step-by-step building must continue at whatever speed best suits the pupil, though he should not be kept at one five-finger group longer than is necessary. If this is done there is a tendency to associate one particular note with its corresponding finger. For the same reason, sight-reading tests should not be too liberally fingered, or the pupil will read from the fingering, instead of from the notes.

In the first stages the intervals should be recognized by their 'shape', beginning with the second, third, and so on. It can be pointed out that the two notes that make up a second (next-door notes) cannot both be on lines or both on spaces, but that those that form a third (next door but one) are on two next-door lines or two next-door spaces. Notice the difference between the appearance of a third and a fifth, and try to get the pupil to read by interval as much as possible. Small chords are easy to recognize, the second having the two notes 'squashed together' and the third, where they 'sit on top of each other'. The 1, 3, 5 chord can be taken in at a glance in the same way.

Teachers may prefer other reading methods than that which begins on Middle C, but the same building process applies, and by whatever method the first notes are learnt, there is no doubt that the lines and spaces must be known in the end. I am not sure whether such sentences as 'Eat Good Bread, Dear Father' give the pupil the right idea; there seems to be something incongruous about them, though I must admit they are never forgotten. I have, on several occasions, come across adults who have said to me: 'I learnt music once, but all I can remember now is "All Cows Eat Grass", or "Every Good Boy Deserves Food".' What a memory to have of one's music lessons! Let us try to do without this if we can. I have found it a good thing to tell the pupil the *first* only of each sequence, and direct him to work the others out for himself, *looking at the keyboard while he does it.* For a little while he may have to continue to look at the keyboard whilst repeating the lines and spaces, but the memorizing will come. coupled with a safe knowledge of the relative positions of the notes. Another way which seems to be fairly successful is to write the lines and spaces in this way:

| Treble lines | E | G B D F | |
| Bass lines | | G B D F | A |

| Treble spaces | F | A C E | |
| Bass spaces | | A C E | G |

The pupil gets a 'visual' idea of them, and notices the close similarity between the treble and bass lines, which have the four central notes in common and, of course, the same likeness between the treble and bass spaces.

Leger lines are taught gradually, though of course Middle C is recognized from the beginning. There is always a tendency for the pupil to play a C for this note ♪ confusing it with Bass Middle C and, similarly, this 𝄢 may be played as C. Explain to the pupil the reason why he is making this mistake, and give a series of reading tests to include the notes in question.

The practice of treating time and rhythm apart from the melody is very good at first. Rhythmic patterns should be clapped at sight whilst the pupil counts the pulses. When time and melody are first combined, the notes should be easy, to enable the pupil to keep up the rhythmic flow.

Having, then, become familiar with the notes and time values, and learnt to find his way about the keyboard, the pupil must learn the most important thing of all about sight-reading, and that is NOT TO LOOK AT THE KEYBOARD. This means not only a good perception of what the printed page conveys, but a good keyboard sense, and exercises should be given in which the pupil plays certain sequences of notes entirely 'by feel'. First of all this is done on a five-notes compass, which is gradually extended. The pupil will enjoy trying to play blindfold, or with his eyes shut, and such things as scales, exercises, and even pieces can be tried in this way. It will all help the sight-reading in the end.

When this stage has been reached the pupil should be encouraged to read as much as possible at home, or in his practice time.

The difficulty here is the outlay on new books, but this can be overcome if the teacher builds up a 'lend and borrow' library. The pupil pays for one new book at the beginning of each term, and when it is finished exchanges it for another. Quite a large sight-reading library can gradually be built up in this way. The scheme is, of course, easier to put into practice in a school, but can also be run successfully by the private teacher, who will find it well worth a small initial outlay to have a few extra books at hand to fall back on. A yearly 'turn-out' is also a good thing. Many pupils are only too willing to hand over old and unwanted music which is lying about at home or filling up the music-case.

During the lesson a lot of fun can be had with duet-playing, or by the pupil reading one hand of a piece while the teacher plays the other. Much of the sight-reading material available does not appeal to the child, particularly the graded tests which are an essential part of examination preparation. They do not stimulate the imagination sufficiently. Books of more attractive pieces of a suitable grade should be substituted whenever possible. A pupil should be able to read pieces about two grades easier than the ones he is actually learning.

One of the most difficult things for young pianists is to 'do nothing', in other words, to wait for rests. It is not realized at first that the pulse of the music is going on all the time, and that the beginning and end of a silence must be as exactly on the beat as the beginning and end of a sound. This is much better appreciated if an example of this kind is played by the teacher:

Ask the pupil to listen to the right hand and describe the number of beats taken up by the rests. Similarly if tied notes are not held for their full value, the following will help:

This time the pupil should describe the length of tied notes *or* rests.

Phrasing is an integral part of music. Even the simplest melody should be phrased. The 'two-phrase' melody can be described as 'Question and Answer', or the terms 'Announcing and Responsive Phrase' used for older beginners. There is nothing more dull and lifeless than the performance of a piece of music in which the phrasing is not shown, and even with beginners there is no need for it to be ignored. The slur is equally important, and should be observed from the time it is first met with. The exercise on page 30 and further remarks on page 123 may help to facilitate the teaching of this.

Fingering, which has to be carefully considered, is often determined by the phrasing. The pupil should be taught to look ahead, try to take in the 'shape' of each phrase and get an imaginary 'feel' of it in his fingers. Fingering can then be chosen that will not make a break in the sequence of notes in a phrase (this will be found more fully explained in the chapter on 'Fingering'). In the first place, the fingering will have to be indicated by the teacher, but it is a very good plan, which the pupil usually enjoys, to give him an unphrased and unfingered piece of music, in which to write the phrasing and fingering.

The key signature is, of course, vitally important: I have dealt with it quite exhaustively in the chapter on scales. We all know that the pupil has to be constantly reminded to look through the piece before attempting it. Clef, key, and time must be observed first, and then follow all the other details according to the grade of the reading. The pupil should 'feel' the rhythm of the first two bars. Once this has been felt there is more likely to be a rhythmical performance throughout. When preparing anyone who is weak in this way for an examination, it is a good plan to pick a number of examples and just hear the first four bars of each.

Fluency is of the greatest importance. To a pupil who is constantly going back to correct wrong notes, it should be pointed out that time and melody are of equal importance, and that to play a wrong note is one mistake, but to go back, and so break the rhythm, is another. On the other hand, of course, faults must be pointed out and corrected. During the lesson the reading should be played through as fluently as possible, and then the teacher should go back with the pupil over the things that have gone wrong. An accidental that occurs more than once in a bar is often missed the second time, tied notes that are part of a chord are seldom noticed, staccato, accents, and marks of expression are all too rarely given their meaning.

At last comes the time when a real attempt at interpretation is made. The music is treated as a whole, the mood felt, the phrases and climaxes made, and the dynamics observed. But it is a long and arduous path, and constant encouragement, coupled with extreme firmness at times, will be needed before this happy state is reached.

The 'Quick Study Test', in which the pupil is given a short piece to learn entirely unaided, is a very good variety of sight-reading. The piece given should be easier than that of the piece the pupil can normally play, and should have incorporated in it some special feature, such as staccato, slurs, tied notes, &c. The pupil brings this to the lesson after a week's practice, and is expected to give an interpretation beyond just the reading of notes. It is an excellent test of general intelligence and musicianship, and is particularly useful in Grade III onwards. It might be given every fourth week in place of sight-reading.

Finally let me stress what I said at the beginning: that the only way to improve in sight-reading is to practise. The growth will be as imperceptible as that of a child, but it will be there, and the achievement will be well worth the hard work.

Here follows a list of books which could well be used as material for sight-reading:

(Music known to be available at time of going to press 1978)

VERY EASY TO GRADE I

Adventures on the New Road	Margery Dawe	Cramer
Come and Play	Donald Forde	Boosey
Simplified Sightreading	Peggy Spencer Palmer	Cramer
Music Makers	Joan Last	Forsyth
Sightreading for the Very Young Pianist	Joan Last	O.U.P.

| *Through the Gateway* | Donald Gray | Boosey |
| *Beginners' Tunes* | Thos. A. Johnson | Hinrichsen |

SERIES GRADED UPWARDS

At the Keyboard	Joan Last	O.U.P.
Play at Sight	Christine Brown	E.M.I.
Rhythmic Reading	Joan Last	Bosworth
Read-Play Series	Thos. A. Johnson	Hinrichsen
Sightreading Tests	Henry Duke	Novello
Sightreading Step by Step	Swinstead	Banks
Pianoforte Sightplaying Exercises	Markham Lee	Chappell

The list quoted above is composed of albums that have been especially written with sightreading in mind. However, the young pianist will benefit by being given 'real books of pieces' to read and this is quite practical after the first stages have been accomplished. As a guide to the grading of these books the average pupil who has reached Grade III in performance should be able to read music of about Grade I in difficulty. Older students enjoy music with which they are familiar and one or two books are suggested here:

Pathway to the Proms	Cyril Dalmaine	Forsyth
The Pianist's Book of Bach Chorales	sel. A. B. Ashby	O.U.P.
Famous Tunes	arr. John Wilson	O.U.P.

Pupil-Teacher duets are also a much enjoyed form of reading. A good series is 'Partners' by Thos. A. Johnson (Hinrichsen).

FINGERING

As long as the pupil is playing music within a five-finger compass, or on five-finger groups, the fingering cannot go very far wrong. As progress is made the fingering requires more and more care. Careless and incorrect fingering should never be passed by the teacher, for it is easier to prevent a fault than to correct it. Good fingering is a matter of habit, and it is in the early years that good or bad habits are formed.

The question which puzzles so many of us is: 'Why, if left to their own devices, do young pianists choose such completely mad fingering?' The only reason I can give is that they are not really bothering about it at all; they have not realized the importance of good fingering, and how much easier things will be if the correct fingering is chosen. The cure lies in the early teaching. As I have just said, five-finger groups seldom present difficulty, and it is only when the compass is extended that the troubles begin.

It is a good plan for the pupil to be invited to co-operate with the teacher in choosing the fingering. A reason must be given for the choice, which can vary only very slightly in easy pieces. When the fingering of a piece has been decided upon, *it must be adhered to*. It is pointed out to the pupil that it is much easier to learn a phrase if it is played through several times with exactly the same fingering. If the fingering is changed the *muscles* are not learning the piece, for it is by *muscular habit* that the constant repetition of the phrase will cause the fingers eventually to play the notes correctly without the conscious direction of the mind.

Though the teacher will have to indicate a great deal of the fingering, let us see what the pupil can do. First of all we will take a simple five-finger group:

The pupil is asked to read this. The intelligent pupil will look at the first *phrase* and realize that it is written on the notes from G to D, and that within this group, B is the middle note; therefore he will start on the middle finger. But for every intelligent pupil there will be many more who will look only at the first *note* and will start on the thumb (or any other finger that comes into their heads). There is a lesson to be learnt from this for the pupil, and this is the first step in the selection of fingering.

In deciding the fingering, the student should consider the music as a series of groups which are shaped to suit the hand. To a certain extent the fingering chosen may vary according to the size of the hand, but on the whole the same rules apply to all. Let us consider the following:

The first example consists of two five-finger groups, therefore the fingering is easy. In the second there is no break in the phrase line, which means that a different fingering will have to be chosen. The group that lies under the hand is marked ⌐――――⌐, which shows us that the change of position comes after the first note.

The two passages that follow will illustrate the same point:

By this we see that the fingering chosen depends largely on the phrasing and continuity of the music. One might turn this round and say that the continuity of the music depends on the correct fingering being used.

Scale passages follow the usual fingering 1, 2, 3—1, 2, 3, 4, and the important point is to determine where the thumb shall come, and which finger shall pass over the thumb.

In the three passages that follow we have to decide which finger shall pass over the thumb at x in each case:

By studying these and similar passages, the student will realize the reason for each choice. It is particularly essential that, in sight-reading, he should learn to look ahead, so that he can make decisions of this kind.

We will now give the pupil a broken chord accompaniment in the left hand:

The key to the fingering of such passages always lies in the shape of the chord played as a whole:

Again, in this type of chord accompaniment the choice of fingering depends on what precedes or follows each group. Consider this example:

Here the C major triad should be fingered as marked (not 5, 3, 1), to shape the hand more easily over the next chord.

The following is similar:

Where chords are marked 'legato', fingering should preserve the legato as nearly as possible. In the two cadences that follow the fingering of the final chord depends on the middle notes in the dominant chord:

When this chord is played in a broken form it is often fingered incorrectly, thereby breaking the quaver line:

In the case of large spread chords it is important that the middle finger should act as a pivot for the thumb and fifth. In practice it should be played first, and an exercise tried out. In this way the pupil will feel whether the correct finger has been chosen:

Where there is an accompaniment of the following type the two chords in a group should be thought of as one, and fingered accordingly:

An exception will have to be made here for small hands, but it is better to avoid over-repetition of $\frac{1}{5}$. The first two chords could be fingered $\frac{1}{5}$, $\frac{1}{4}$, &c.

It is not usual to play the thumb on a black key in scale or arpeggio passages that go straight up or down, but where there are chords, the thumb falls into its natural position whether the notes are black or white. This also applies to small groups of broken chords. The following will illustrate where two similar passages are transposed into another key.

First, a scale passage. The fingering of the second one is changed on account of the black key:

Now a broken chord passage. The fingering is the same in both keys:

In sequential passages each similar group of notes should have, as far as possible, the same fingers on the corresponding notes, the thumb taking its place regardless of whether the key is black or white.

The speed of a piece will in some cases determine the fingering. The following will illustrate:

It will be seen in the second of the last two examples that, at *, the fingers are changed on a note that is held down. This will often be necessary in contrapuntal music, especially where one hand plays more than one part. It can be practised by means of exercises like the following:

using different combinations of fingers. Or:

Sometimes it will be found necessary to slide the finger from a black to white note. It is possible to maintain a legato while doing so if it is practised carefully. The following will help:

As the pupil advances he will learn the need for passing the third or fourth fingers *over* the little finger. He should be able to play a scale with varied fingerings:

Left Hand similarly in contrary motion (starting on C)

The last one is a good preparation for legato octaves, where the fourth is used.

Staccato passages that lie in groups under the hand, or that go straight up and down, should have the same fingering as if they were legato. This also applies to groups of chords, but where there are skips the fingering may be different.

When a note is repeated several times at speed the finger should be changed. It is easier, and more correct technically, to use the fingers from the outside inwards, thus:

To a large extent technique and fingering are complementary to one another. Where the technique is good, and the hands are well shaped and controlled, it is more likely that the fingers will fall into their natural places in each group. Where they stick out in all directions it is obvious that anything may happen, and often does! Similarly, well-chosen fingering shapes the hand into balanced groups over the keyboard, whereas badly chosen fingering causes the fingers to go into ugly unnatural positions in their efforts to get hold of the notes.

It is a good plan to give an occasional test in which the pupil writes the fingering and brings it to the next lesson, as was suggested in the chapter on 'Sight-reading'. There is no better way of making him realize that thought is required in this important part of his practising.

The teacher should discuss the fingering of a new piece that is given *before* it is practised by the pupil. This need not be a hard-and-fast rule, but where the pupil is inexperienced it is far the best course. If this is not done, much of the first week's practising may have to be undone and the fingering corrected. It should only be necessary to write a finger here and there in such places as the beginning of a phrase, the passage of the thumb, and extended chord, but this will depend on the pupil. Some seem to have no idea of the most obvious points, and in their case much firmness and patience will be needed.

The main thing is for a pupil to be given a reason for everything he does not understand, so as to form good habits during the first few years of music lessons.

N.B.—An excellent book on fingering is that of Thomas B. Knott entitled *Pianoforte Fingering* (O.U.P.).

PEDALLING

THE pedals are seldom used in the early lessons, but there is no reason why they should be avoided altogether after the preliminary stages have been passed. There are quite a number of really easy educational pieces in which, under the careful guidance of the teacher, a little judicious use of the pedal would add greatly to the effect. The one difficulty is that smaller children cannot reach the ground with their feet, which causes them to use the pedal incorrectly. In their case, unless a special attachment is available, it would be better to leave it for the present.

Before using either pedal the pupil should understand what effect they will have on the sound and how this effect is produced. First the pupil should look inside the piano and see

whathappens when the teacher uses one or other of the pedals.
It must be understood that the right-hand pedal is *not* called
the 'loud' pedal. This idea is very prevalent, and, though it is
true it does intensify the sound, yet, it can be demonstrated,
it is possible to play very softly with this pedal in action, or
even to use it at the same time as the soft pedal. First, then,
the word 'sustain' should be explained, and the pupil shown
how the action of the pedal sustains the sound by lifting the
dampers from the strings. In this way the pupil will understand the meaning of its real name: 'the sustaining pedal' or
'damper pedal'.

It can have three different effects upon the sound: First, it
enriches the quality of the tone and increases the sustaining
power. To demonstrate this the teacher plays a chord,
holding it down for about eight counts, first with and then
without the pedal.

It is a mystery at first that the notes fade more easily when
the pedal is not held down, for the dampers are in any case
held away from the notes as long as the key is pressed down.
An interesting experiment is for the teacher to play a chord
again, holding it for a greater number of bars, and pedalling
as indicated:

The pupil with a sensitive ear will notice that each time
the pedal goes down there appear to be other sounds or harmonies besides those originally played, and that when the
pedal comes up, those sounds disappear and the original notes
sound thin. This enriching of the sound is caused by the
'sympathetic vibration' of other notes that are in harmony
with the first chord.

A further experiment is to play a note or small chord
silently, pressing the keys so gently that no sound is made.
The pedal is depressed at the same time. This is held whilst

an arpeggio is played, extending from bass to treble of the keyboard. When the arpeggio is finished the pedal is released and the original chord is still held down. It will be found that the notes are now singing. Their strings have been set into vibration by the notes of the arpeggio.

These experiments will show that the pedal needs careful intelligent use, or we may get a number of vibrations that are *not* harmonious.

The second thing the pedal can do is to join sounds which cannot be reached by the hands:

The third is to make several notes sound on together, which has already been demonstrated in the second 'experiment'.

Now it is for the pupil to use the pedal. He should first of all practise without the hands. This may seem to him a funny thing to do, but it is very important to learn exactly how much pressure is needed on the pedal and how far it should be taken up. The heel *must* be on the ground, and the sole of the foot (not the toe) should maintain contact with the pedal for as long as it is in use (see Plate VIII, Fig. 1, facing p. 101). If the foot is lifted too high it falls back on to the pedal with an audible tapping sound which can be most annoying. If the pedal is allowed to come up too suddenly its mechanism will cause it to make a 'bang', which can be equally annoying. These faults are sometimes evident in the pedalling of advanced pianists; I have even heard a professional do this in a recital. Unfortunately, the sound seems to be blotted out to the ears of the performer, and only becomes noticeable as it travels down the room.

It will be seen, then, how important it is to start the right way and to develop the habit of listening very carefully to the effects of the pedal. No two pedals have exactly the same weight and response and, because of this, extra care has to be taken when playing on a strange piano. I once heard an adjudicator say: 'You pedal with your ears'. How very true that is! When we learn to play our first notes on the piano we listen to what we are doing with our fingers; now we are going to listen to what we are doing with our feet.

Having got used to the 'feel' of the pedal and gauged the correct amount of movement to control it, the pupil pedals, while the teacher plays :

These progressions can be played by the teacher whilst the pupil sits in his usual place facing the centre of the keyboard.

Legato pedalling (the joining of several chords or groups of notes) is not attempted yet. At this stage the pedal is introduced in pieces where it can enhance the effect without appreciably altering the grade of difficulty. Here are examples of easy pieces where this would be possible:

The Little Chimney Sweep
from *Tales from Hans Andersen* by Yvonne Adair. (O.U.P.)

(Hand and foot come up together as the phrase ends.)

The Lonely Track
from *Downland* by Joan Last. (O.U.P.)

Gliding Swans
from *Kensington Gardens* by Ruby Holland. (O.U.P.)

Little Miss Muffet
from *Nursery Portraits* by Arthur Baynon. (O.U.P.)
(Last five bars)

We now have to learn to bring the pedal into a phrase of this kind:

If the foot goes down at the *same* moment as the chord, the notes of the previous beat will be caught in the sound. This is because, in a true legato, one key is not released until the new sound is made. The pupil now has to learn to make the sound first and then press the pedal down to sustain it. In the preliminary exercise for this it is a good thing to take an example where there is plenty of time and count thus (putting the pedal down *on* 2):

When this lesson has been learnt the pedal can be introduced in another way:

Here the pedal will have to go down just after the first beat, *not with it*. It must be released on the second beat with the end of slur.

Finally we come to legato changes, which will need much care and perseverance in practice. The teacher will find it worth while to 'get down to earth' and control the pupil's foot with her hand during the first lesson (see Plate VIII,

Fig. 2). A very easy chord sequence should be given, so that
the pupil can concentrate on the pedal movements. Again
we get the 'down' movement on 'two', but this time there is
an 'up' movement on 'one'.

Easy pieces with slow chords are now used for practice,
and gradually the 'down' movement is incorporated with the
'up' movement, so that at each pedal change the pupil
thinks 'up–down'.

Evening
from *Tunes for Everyone* by Doreen Fifer (O.U.P.)

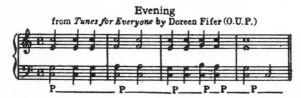

Hymn-tunes also provide plenty of material for practice.
When the pupil can successfully pedal a series of legato
chords, the same principle is applied to a broken harmony,
with a bass of this kind:

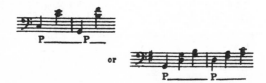

Here the pedal-changes must be quicker and neater, but it
must always be remembered that the pedal *comes up* on the
first beat of the new harmony and goes down immediately
afterwards. The pupil must make sure that he does not leave
go of the lower bass harmony with his finger before it has
been 'caught' by the pedal. It can be shown that the

PLATE VII

Fig. 1.—Incorrect hand position for clapping

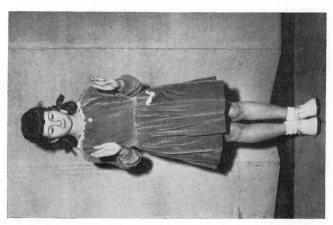

Fig. 2.—Correct hand position for clapping

PLATE VIII

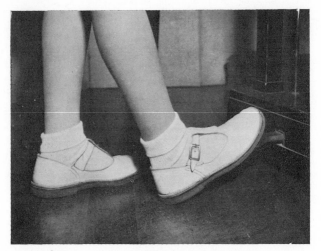

Fig. 1.—Correct position of foot on pedal

Fig. 2.—Showing how the teacher can control the pedal
(this is normally done from the right-hand side)

momentary return of the damper on to the string will cause that particular note to be 'lost'.

Next we come to broken chords. Again the footwork must be even neater and more accurate. The exact moment for the change can be determined only by listening critically.

As the pupil progresses he will need to use the sustaining pedal more and more frequently. One cannot lay down the law as to when it shall be used, that depends so very much on the skill of the performer. The early contrapuntal works were written for an instrument which had no such device as the sustaining pedal, and it is therefore possible to give a performance of them without its use. At the same time it is generally admitted that many such works, especially those with slow-moving parts, are considerably enhanced by its use. I have written about this extensively in my book for more advanced players: *Interpretation for the Piano Student*. I would also recommend, for further study, *Pedalling the Modern Pianoforte* by York Bowen (O.U.P.). These books take up the subject where the early lessons given here leave off.

The young pianist, who has not reached the advanced stages, should at all times be guided by the teacher in matters of pedalling. Later he will learn how to gain effects by the addition of pedal in brilliant scale passages which, at a slow speed, would sound most unpleasant.

Modern composers demand special effects from the use of the pedal, and sometimes comparatively easy pieces will have indications for pedalling marked by them. These should be adhered to, or, if the teacher does not wish the pupil to use the pedal, a piece of this kind should not be given. In any **case, the pupil cannot be expected to pedal well without care-**

ful and systematic teaching, and this is a most important part of the piano lesson.

Whereas many modern composers indicate their wishes with regard to pedalling, there are editions of classical works which have pedal-marks that are completely misleading. Over and over again one sees the sign * (take the pedal up) at the end of each bar, followed by 'put it down' at the beginning of the next bar. Were the student to follow this correctly he would get the most unsatisfactory results, not only because it is wrong, but because no piece should be pedalled in the same way from bar to bar with monotonous regularity.

Fortunately many editions which are available today are the work of thinking pianists and we find such details more clearly presented. In choosing music for our pupils these points need to be borne in mind. It would be better to use copies with no pedal marks than those that are misleading.

The intelligent pupil may ask how it is that the pedal can have an effect in the higher registers of the piano when these strings have no dampers. He will be reminded of the 'sympathetic vibration', which the action of the pedal sets up when these notes are played. At the same time he should notice how the lower and thicker strings of the piano sing for longer after they have been struck, and, because of this, they should not be damped out with such a quick pedal action as the higher strings.

These little points help to keep the student interested in the cause and effect of all things that are done in piano-playing. He is more likely to work with interest if reasons are given for everything that he is asked to do.

In the case of the soft pedal, its action is less easy to demonstrate, owing to the variety of different mechanisms used on the upright piano. The pupil who practises on a grand piano is fortunate.

At the lesson (assuming it is on a grand piano) the pupil is shown how, when the soft pedal is pressed down, the keyboard and action move sideways. This causes the hammer to strike two strings instead of three, and, incidentally, the softer, less worn part of the felt comes into use. It is explained that at one time, when there were two strings to each note, the action of the soft pedal caused the hammer to strike one of the two. So we get the term 'una corda', which means 'one string'. On an upright piano the most usual mechanism is for the soft-pedal action to move the hammers nearer to the strings. In this way they strike them more gently.

If the music is marked 'pp' it does not necessarily mean that the soft pedal is to be used. It is reserved for special effects when the peculiar tonal quality which it can produce is needed. For this reason it is not often required in the earlier Grades.

There are no complicated changes to learn, as in the case of the sustaining pedal. It is simply held down for the duration of the passage in which its effect is to be made.

PRACTISING

DURING the lesson the teacher is constantly telling the pupil to practise this or practise that, but very often the pupil has no idea *how* to practise this or that. Considering the amount of time spent at the piano away from any supervision, it is most essential that some trouble should be taken over teaching methods of practice.

The first thing which the child has to learn is, that *practice means repetition.* I am reminded of a little girl from Poland who came to a school with which I am connected. She had already had some piano lessons, and was sent to a music-room to practise. After seven or eight minutes she reappeared, and on it being suggested to her that she could not yet have finished, she replied: 'I play one hand, I play other hand, I play two hands, I finish'. This will be the attitude of many children towards practising unless they have some definite plan on which to work.

It is through repetition that music is learnt. There was a time when we first learnt to tie a shoelace, and it required great concentration and effort. After a while the action became a muscular habit, and we did not have to think about it any more. So it is with piano-playing: if we play a phrase enough times the fingers learn to do it automatically, without the conscious direction of the brain. This does not mean that the brain becomes inactive—far from it—but it is left free to concentrate on the interpretative side of the music. We then become something like a conductor who directs an orchestra. The fingers are the orchestra who play the notes for us, and we direct *how* they shall be played. We determine the speed, the tone, the nuance, and so on. To achieve these things the orchestra may need many rehearsals, so that the instrumentalists (the fingers) can feel the conditions required to gain the exact effect we want. So, once more, it is a case of repetition until that effect has been achieved.

The experienced musician reads into the music and strives to interpret it from the start. Where it is technically difficult he practises those passages until they have been perfected. The beginner is completely taken up with learning the notes, and suggestions for expression may have to come from the teacher. Between these two extremes we get the gradual merging of note-reading with musical intuition. It is here that the difference between the musical and unmusical child is the most noticeable. The musical child will feel the impulse of the music and (unconsciously perhaps) convey something of it to the listener without being taught. The unmusical child will see before him a series of notes and time values which have to be played. Again, there are many differences between these two extremes.

How, then, can we teach the child to practise? At first a great deal is done at the lesson. Phrases are repeated many times until they have been learnt by the fingers, and the pupil is made to realize that this repetition is essential when learning anything new. It must not only be note repetition, but a repetition of tonal effects. Phrasing, staccato, accents, crescendos, rallentandos are observed and repeated until they are felt correctly.

Often the child will come to a lesson with a page of music very nearly perfect, but spoilt by one or two bad stumbles, which always occur in the same places. This is typical of the pupil who starts to practise his piece at the beginning and goes straight through several times, repeating the same mistakes at each performance. It does not seem to dawn on him to tackle these difficulties first, until the suggestion has come from the teacher. First he must get to the root of the trouble ; it may be wrong fingering, or a phrase that does not lie comfortably under the hand. There may be a chord which has to be 'hunted for', or a group of notes that are technically difficult. Whatever the difficulty, the pupil must be shown that it should be dealt with first, and repeated many times until the fingers get the feel of it. When this has been done the piece is played from the beginning, though it may take several practices before the difficulties are overcome.

The chief thing is for the pupil to learn to use his time wisely, giving the most to the things that need it. Some teachers like to divide the practice up and allocate so many minutes to each part. This means that the pupil practises 'to the clock', and it does not leave any room for his own initiative. It is better to divide the work into sections and make it clear which section should receive the most attention, or which will only need to be revised.

A very important form of practice is SLOW practice. The quicker and more brilliant a passage the more it will need to be practised slowly. Even when well known, certain sections will need a daily dose of slow practice if they are not to get 'out of hand'. If runs are uneven it will be found helpful to play them with varying accents. Passages consisting of broken chords, particularly bass accompaniments such as the following:

should be repeated with the accent first on the first note of the group, then on the second followed by the third and fourth each in turn. Students tend to hurry the last two notes of such groups, and another excellent form of practice is to pass the group from beat to beat, in this way:

(Repeat several times, then extend towards next beat and continue as before.)

Where there is a long phrase of continuous quavers or semiquavers the less advanced pupil will have difficulty in maintaining the continuity. It will be found helpful if it is practised in groups at first, and the groups gradually joined up. This passage from one of the 'Anna Magdalena' pieces of Bach is typical:

First it should be divided into phrases, and each phrase repeated several times:

Then the phrases are put together, two at a time. Finally the whole passage is played slowly, making sure that the phrasing remains. Needless to say, such a passage will need careful fingering, which is indicated by the teacher at the beginning.

From the first lesson the pupil should have a note-book in which is written the work that has to be done. At first everything is given in detail, including reminders about sitting posture, arm and finger action, and so on. Directions are included for note finding and naming, and for practising technical exercises. The section of music which has to be read or learnt is written down, with reminders as to note values or rests. As the pupil progresses, new work is added and noted —the first scale, the position of the semitones, key signatures, new time values, expression marks, and so on.

It must be remembered that to *say* a thing is not enough; the child has a great deal to take in and remember, and it will be much easier if everything is written down.

In setting the work many things have to be taken into consideration, and a pupil should never be given more than he can manage. Before very long the teacher will be able to assess the amount of which he is capable. She must also consider the time that is available for practice. Children who are at school have a very full life, and practising may be limited by school work or home conditions. Temporary emergencies sometimes arise, such as school examinations or illness at home, and it is unreasonable to expect the usual amount of work at such times. If the teacher is considerate, and does not treat the pupil like a machine, he is far more likely to co-operate and give his best.

The enthusiastic pupil will 'make time' which, for others, does not exist. In his enthusiasm he may practise far beyond the work that has been set, bringing pages of a rather sketchy performance instead of the one page which has been given. This enthusiasm should not be discouraged, but he must be made to see that, to practise two lines until they are perfect will, in the long run, get him further than to play two pages with the same mistakes each time. In his case a certain section is set, to be learnt first, and a further section to be included if time remains. The teacher should go through the details beforehand, marking any fingering, or points that will need extra care. She should also give him plenty of supplementary material for reading.

Finally we come to the problem: 'How can I *make* my pupils practise?' We all know what it is like to have a pupil who brings the same mistakes lesson after lesson, and how the feeling of exasperation rises as the weeks go by. The question is 'Why does he bring the same mistakes?' There *may* be a reason, but we know that, very often, it is just laziness. However, we must be sure of this; for there may be other contributory causes. Are we sure that the piece is not too difficult? Are we sure that the proper conditions are provided for practice? Are we sure that the child has understood exactly what we want, or that he knows *how* to practise?

The difference between one pupil and another is quite amazing, and I do not want my readers to think that every suggestion made throughout this book is infallible. We always come up against the human element, which can be stronger than all the methods in the world. It is quite clear that, with these difficult pupils, it is no use just 'getting cross' *every* lesson. They simply dig their heels in and get more and more difficult. I have often found that a challenge to their ability can be very effective. In this case the teacher takes the blame on herself, saying that she is afraid she has chosen something much too difficult, and promising to look out an easier piece by the next lesson. She produces one or two examples (as dull as possible!) of the sort of thing he might try, but finds she cannot spare a copy until next week. By next week it is more than likely a miraculous change will have taken place, and the easy piece will not be needed!

Again I have found it very effective to let them 'get along with it' for one lesson, explaining that, as it is rather waste of time to say the same things again, they must play the piece their own way. This negative attitude from the teacher means a very boring lesson, and the pupil will soon realize he would rather be corrected than just left to stumble on.

One will come across children who have made up their minds that they will never be any good. Very often they are comparing themselves with someone else who is particularly quick, or there may be brothers and sisters who say: 'Can't you play anything else? I'm fed up with that piece'. These children must be given every possible encouragement. Whatever it is that they do well must be made much of. Perhaps they have good hands and a nice touch. The teacher should tell them that this is one of the best things to have, for they can make the notes sound beautiful, which is the thing that really matters. This encouragement leads to renewed efforts with sight-reading and learning, and before long they have lost the feeling of hopelessness.

Ensemble playing is a great incentive to practice, and an excellent training in musicianship. Piano duets are the most usual form of ensemble playing for young people, and there is often a certain amount of healthy rivalry between partners, which does no harm, but merely spurs them on to greater effort. Here the learning of the notes is only a means to an end, and the two pianists will realize that they cannot even begin to play together until each has practised his own part well.

Even with small children infinite pains should be taken in the matter of balance and ensemble. It is never too early for young musicians to be taught to listen for these things. They have to listen not only to themselves, but to each other, and to get the greatest benefit from this experience they should practise regularly together.

It is interesting to give two young pianists a duet to learn and practise together, putting their own ideas into it—I often feel I would like to be a fly on the wall during these practices, which occasionally are quite stormy affairs when opinions on interpretation differ!—Usually it will be found that one child takes the lead and the other recognizes the leadership, and co-operates. Once they have grasped the main essentials of duet-playing, children will throw themselves wholeheartedly into this type of practising, and are full of ideas and suggestions.

Two-piano playing is an even more satisfying form of partnership, and those who have the opportunity to work at it are very fortunate.

Later the pianist should be encouraged to search for friends who sing, or play another instrument, so that his musical experience gradually widens. The piano can be a very lonely instrument, and we must see to it that the pupil is able to work with others in some way or other before he has progressed very far.

The teacher must learn to get a sense of proportion when judging the work done by various pupils. It must always be remembered that comparisons are dangerous things. Each pupil should be considered on his own merits, for what will mean hard work to one is quite easy to another. It is very difficult indeed to be absolutely fair in the matters of praise or censure, but this is one of the things that we must strive after. It is disappointing for a pupil who has practised well, and overcome some difficulty, to have his success overlooked. The teacher has to remember what happened at the last lesson, so that she can realize the progress made. Once more let me stress that the 'practice book' not only tells the pupil what to do, but reminds the teacher of what she has set. This is the most important thing of all, for there must be a clear understanding between teacher and pupil.

Part Three

FROM STUDENT TO ARTIST

INTRODUCTION TO PART THREE

THE concert artist, in his performance, gives an interpretation which is imbued with his own personality. It is a reading of the work which is a result of his experience, and its degree of perfection is qualified by his technical skill and sense of artistry.

The child playing his first piece has, as yet, no musical experience and little skill, but he has imagination, and it is through this that he learns his first lessons in interpretation.

The first pieces, as have been illustrated earlier in the book, will have to be very simple; for no child can give a performance unless the playing is fluent, and fluency cannot be attained if the playing of the notes is a struggle.

Fluency, then, is the first step towards artistry and interpretation. The greatest obstacle that stands in its way, at whatever Grade, is poor technique. One might truly say: 'The spirit is willing but the fingers are weak', and the child who has a natural sense of artistry will be the first to admit that he cannot get the effect he wants because his fingers 'won't do it'.

Besides the ordinary technical problems with which the beginner is faced, there are other more subtle things which have to be learnt as the repertoire increases.

The details of legato, staccato, slurs, accents, and so on are as important now as they will ever be. Each new problem and difficulty must be tackled as it arises, so that a really good foundation can be laid for the interpretative faculty to develop. The pupil very quickly learns to appreciate these finer points and to understand the difference they can make to the sound of a piece. Whilst these details are being taught, no piece should be given that is beyond the technical ability of the pupil, or these finer points of artistry will be lost in a struggle to 'learn the notes'.

COMMON FAULTS—THEIR ANTICIPATION
AND PREVENTION

THERE are certain difficulties with which the experienced teacher is familiar. These are faults which crop up again and again, and which turn into bad habits if they are not dealt with and checked from the start. It has been said that prevention is better than cure, and, with this in mind, let us discuss some of the things that will probably happen, and see how they can be prevented. It is easier to take them one by one under separate headings.

1. *Inability to Synchronize the Hands*

When the pupil begins to play hands together, we must make sure that they really *are* together. Every now and then a beginner will have difficulty in putting down a note in each hand at precisely the same moment. The left hand usually precedes the right, perhaps only by a fraction, but the smallest fraction should never be ignored. It can develop into a chronic and almost incurable fault.

It is rather difficult to deal with, because one seems to be constantly 'nagging' at the pupil. It can only be cured by critical listening on the part of the pupil. The teacher should demonstrate by playing some notes correctly, and 'splitting' some, so that the pupil can hear the difference. He should say, in each case, whether the teacher played correctly or not. Having *heard* the mistake, it is up to the pupil to correct it, though of course at lessons it should be checked every time it happens. Not very long ago a small boy came to me for lessons. He had reached Grade II, and yet was not able to play his scales with the hands dead together. We managed to cure the fault fairly quickly. He would play a scale while I shut my eyes and counted the number of split notes. At the first lesson there were twenty-nine (every note), at the second about half the number, in four weeks' time there were three, and then none. Even after this triumph he used sometimes to start a scale, and, after a few notes, exclaim 'Oh no', and go back to the beginning. It was his sense of self-criticism and the realization of his fault that won the battle.

If it appears to be a really serious difficulty, the pupil should try playing each note with a little added arm-weight working the arms exactly together, and repeating each note several times.

Anyone who has a weakness in this direction will need careful guidance when he reaches the stage where both hands play chords (in the style of a hymn tune), and the fault may also crop up again in a piece of this type, where the left hand moves down on the first beat of each bar:

For some unknown reason there will again be a tendency to play the left hand first at *.

It is possible that this tendency is a 'throw-back' from our harpsichord-playing ancestors, who, having no adequate sustaining device, 'split' the chords for greater resonance. The habit was still quite fashionable in the very early part of the twentieth century.

2. *Breaking up the Legato Line*

Many early pieces have phrases in which the melodic line is passed from one hand to the other in this way:

Each of the two phrases in the last example should, to the listener, sound exactly as though it were being played in one hand. With the beginner, however, there is often difficulty here. There may either be a break in the continuity of the sound at *, or the first hand may be held down beyond the entrance of the second hand, giving an effect something like this:

The pupil will be able to hear the difference between the correct and incorrect performances if they are demonstrated by the teacher, but it may be necessary to improvise exercises for practice in getting the join exactly right in his own performance.

A melody could be given which can be played in two different ways:

    1. In one hand.

    2. Divided between the hands.

The pupil practises it these two ways under the guidance of the teacher. When the join has been successfully achieved, the teacher shuts her eyes and listens. If the pupil makes the join correctly, the teacher will be unable to tell whether he is playing it with both hands or one hand.

The next problem is to preserve the legato line in a piece of this type:

PLATE IX

Duet-playing is excellent training in musicianship

PLATE X

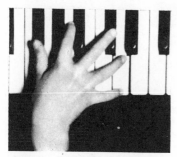

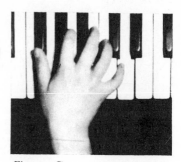

Fig. 1.—Incorrect approach to
the F ♯ A chord
(See musical context, page 126)

Fig. 2.—Correct approach to the
same chord

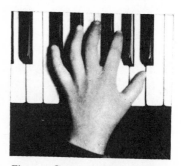

Fig. 3.—Incorrect approach to
the C ♯ G chord
(See musical context, page 126)

Fig. 4.—Correct approach to the
same chord

At first glance it looks no harder than an early example on page 35. But notice the long, unbroken phrase line in the right-hand melody. At the first attempt it is very likely that it will be broken up like this:

This disjointedness is entirely wrong—it is just as wrong as playing the incorrect notes. It cannot be emphasized too strongly that to allow the pupil to continue with this kind of fault is laying the very worst foundations. To play the right hand legato throughout and keep the tune singing on while the left hand lifts before each chord is often difficult at first, but the difficulty can be surmounted very quickly if tackled the right way.

First of all the right hand should be played alone very legato—listening to the 'song'. (The teacher could also play it with breaks in the continuity, for the pupil to detect.) Next, after making sure of the left hand chords, the hands should be put together in this way:

Naturally the pauses should be dispensed with as soon as possible, but at first they are useful to the teacher, who can, for example, during the first pause, instruct the pupil to 'lift' the left hand while playing the next note with the right, and during the second pause tell the pupil now to prepare the next chord and then play both hands exactly together, *keeping the right hand legato all the time*. It is the 'taking-off' of the left hand in time to play again on the first beat of the next bar that solves the problem. At first the left hand is better played as a dotted minim with a crotchet rest for the 'lift'— later the 'lift' may come a little later, but in actual fact the semibreve could never be given its full value. If the 'lift' is left until 'one' of the next bar, the hasty jerk required to put down the next chord causes disjointedness in the rhythm, and there is a momentary stiffness of the muscles, which causes the right hand to react to the left-hand movement and lose its continuity.

All the above instructions are not as slow and tedious as they sound, and are well worth the trouble.

Another type of piece requiring the same kind of treatment is this:

Care should be taken that the legato accompaniment of the left hand is not broken. The same kind of practice may be needed before this can be correctly played.

The following simple exercise will be found useful for gaining independence between the hands:

Another thing that sometimes causes a break in the continuity of the legato line is the entry of the accompanying hand in the middle of a phrase:

In the above example it is possible that the beginner will make a break in the right-hand melody at *. This is not difficult to correct, and it will usually be sufficient for the teacher to play it the right and wrong way for the pupil to hear the difference. Those who find any difficulty should practise having the left hand in readiness, touching the keys, so that only a gentle pressure is needed when the time comes. In some cases it may be necessary to practise this:

several times first.

Where the phrase does not begin on the first beat of the bar, and the first beat is approached by an anacrusis in one hand alone, the same thing will have to be watched for. Make sure that the rhythm is felt beforehand, and that the left hand is ready with its accompanying chord:

3. *The Phrase*

Having learnt to play legato, we must not forget that the smooth continuity of sound can only be effective if it is 'within the phrase'. In teaching this to young children it can be likened to a song in which the singer takes a breath before each new phrase. The teacher should demonstrate with a passage of this kind, which could be both played and sung:

It should also be shown on the piano how monotonous the passage would sound if the 'musical breaths' were not taken.

The right technical action for the ending or beginning of a phrase is easier to make if it is likened to a breath *in preparation* for a new phrase. It is not so much a 'rest' as a releasing of the weight from the keys, and pupils should not be allowed to make exaggerated movements to indicate beginning and ends of phrases.

Many editions of music, especially those of the classics, have phrase-marks which are vague in the extreme. In choosing music this should be carefully considered. Copies with no phrasing are better than those with bad phrasing, for, in these, the teacher can write what she considers is suitable.

The word 'phrasing' also applies to the smaller subdivisions within the phrase and the details of staccato, legato, the slur, and so on.

4. *Staccato—Failure to Observe It and Faulty Anticipation*

Staccato, as such, with simple exercises for teaching it, has already been mentioned earlier in this book. The following does not deal with the technical side of staccato.

Many pupils seem to be unable to realize that when a

composer marks a passage staccato, *he means it*, and the whole character of the piece is changed if it is ignored. He also means just as many staccato notes, neither more nor less, as are marked in the music. It is a fact that quite three-quarters of the pianists in their early stages, who meet this sort of thing:

will play it thus:

or, if there are three staccato notes, as in:

it will be played as:

There is no particular method of curing this fault, as it only needs thought on the part of the pupil, and untiring firmness on the part of the teacher, who should *never once* let it pass. It may persist in quite advanced pupils if not carefully watched.

The same kind of thing occurs, when a legato melody is accompanied by staccato chords:

The result is often:

To cure this make the second chord lighter.

When a staccato note is preceded by a series of legato notes:

it is often found that the pupil checks the approach to the staccato note by 'anticipating' the staccato—i.e. by making a break, or a gap, between the staccato note and the preceding one, thus:

This is still more likely to happen if the left hand enters as the staccato note is played.

This phrase:

becomes:

This tendency has already been mentioned earlier, and the continuous practice of the 'Run and Jump' or similar exercises should put things right, provided that it is applied whenever similar phrases are met with.

5. *The Difficulties of the Slur*

The slur is a difficult sign to teach, and is frequently ignored. Simple exercises, such as those in the chapter on 'Early Technique,' pave the way technically, but they have yet to be recognized and interpreted from the written page. The pupil has to understand that this:

means approximately:

and, furthermore, that the degree of crispness of the notes here marked staccato depends on the context and mood of the piece, and is governed by the music that precedes or follows it. This needs more experience than the child can muster, and the teacher must carefully explain and illustrate the slur on all occasions with which it is met, so that experience will gradually be gained.

The following examples will illustrate:

This is a gay dancing piece, and here the G should be short and crisp, to match the staccato notes which follow it.

Here is another example of the slur:

In this case the B and G crotchets should not be taken off abruptly. They should 'float off' with the tone carefully graded to match the 'fading off' of the minim which precedes them.

We also must realize that the last note in a slur is not always the softest. It depends on whether it is written from a strong to a weak beat (as in the examples just given) or from weak to strong, as in the following:

Here, with the slur ending on the strong beat, it should come off with a 'kick', so that the accents are in keeping with the rhythmic measures:

Several notes may be grouped together within the slur, and the same rules apply:

to be played as:

Or, again from weak to strong:

to be played as:

Where the slur line extends to a note which comes on a strong beat and ends a group or phrase, then that note is given its full value:

In the above the chord at * takes its full value, whilst the slur at + is treated as staccato.

In the above the chords at * take their full value, whilst the slur at + comes off gently.

6. *Awkward Hand Position, and Lack of Anticipation*

Often a break in the continuity of the music will be caused by a note in a chord which does not conveniently lie under the hand. Usually it is a chord in which the thumb or fifth finger plays a black key, and for which the whole hand needs to be further forward on the keyboard. The beginner tries to make this adjustment of the hand at the last moment, the result being a sudden jerk. To overcome this jerk, the chord and new hand position should be anticipated in plenty of time, and the notes preceding the chord should be played *well forward* on the keys:

In the previous example the hand should begin to prepare for the F sharp A chord at × the position at ⌐ being as though this chord was being played  (see Plate X, Figs. 1 and 2, facing p. 117). Here is a further example:

At × the hand should be in position over the complete chord  (see Plate X, Figs. 3 and 4, facing p. 117). In the following the whole passage should be played well forward on the keys, especially the third finger at *:

7. *The Broken Line in Legato Chords (without the Use of the Pedal)*

In dealing with the slur it was only mentioned in connection with the single melodic line. When chords are slurred the practising of such sequences as the following is helpful:

These can be played ascending or descending, and similarly in the left hand. Technically they are not difficult, provided there is relaxation. The first chord of each phrase should be slightly accented and played with more arm-weight than those that follow.

Following on from this, we might get a sequence of legato chords, such as:

Everything here is quite straightforward up to the last three chords. Here a flexible thumb is required, which can be lifted between its repetitions without the legato of the upper part being broken. Progressions such as the following are often incorrectly played, owing to inability to preserve the legato whilst the thumb is replayed:

If the difficulty persists, slow practice is required. The pupil should be told to play the first chord and then wait. Then, carefully raise the thumb, but *not* the other note (this should sing on). Now place the thumb and finger into position over the next chord. Then, using the weight of the arm to help, transfer the sound from the singing note (or held note) to the second chord. This should be done several times.

It is not always the thumb that has the repeated notes. Other progressions should be practised in the same way. There must always be continuity of sound between the parts which can be played legato.

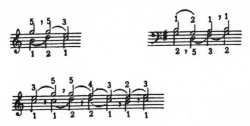

The anticipation and correction of so many faults may seem rather a formidable task, but it is not usual for any one pupil to have them all. In any case they are dealt with, one by one, as they are encountered, and the attitude to them should be not so much that they are faults, but that the pupil is taking another step forward in his knowledge of piano-playing. If this seems to be 'begging the point', I would say that there is a world of difference between destructive and constructive criticism. Things *can* be put to the pupil in such a way that he feels he is continually doing wrong, *or* in a way that makes him feel he is learning and accomplishing something new.

A big problem for the teacher is the new pupil who comes to her having learnt previously, and who has been allowed to do just those things we are trying to prevent. It is much more difficult to cure a bad habit than to prevent it forming, and a great deal of patience will be needed to deal with it. It is obvious that the pupil will become discouraged if the teacher is constantly stopping and correcting him. The biggest mistake is to go back and try to put right those pieces he has already learnt. Entirely new work should be given, chosen so that the worst of his weaknesses can be encountered and dealt with first. These pieces may have to be easier than those he has been learning, and it can be explained to him that, now he has got so far, the time has come for him to learn more about the details which go into the performance of a piece. It is better to start with something in which the notes are easy, so that he can think about the new ideas he is going to put into them.

The difficulties will then be dealt with in the way I have previously outlined, though the teacher may have to be less strict over smaller faults while the main essentials are being dealt with.

As in all branches of piano-playing, the pupil will learn a great deal through critical listening and imitation. The teacher should demonstrate the various manners of performance and ask him to say which he prefers, and why.

If we can lay the foundations of good habits in piano-playing, then we can be sure that the pupil will not lose them as he progresses. It is worth taking endless trouble over these small things, for they are not really small in the eyes of the artist, and no performance can be really pleasing and polished unless they have been attended to.

THE PATHWAY TO INTERPRETATION

'INTERPRETATION in music is simply the act of performance.' So says Percy Scholes in *The Oxford Companion to Music*. It could not be more clearly put.

Interpretation in its most advanced stages cannot be taught, but those things which will enable the performer to give an interpretation can be indicated as he progresses.

Supposing, then, that we are teaching our pupils to 'Give a performance' of an easy piece. This performance should contain something more than just correctness. What else are we going to try to put into it? By what merits would an audience judge its interpretation? Here are some things I would suggest:

> Choice of Tempo.
> A feeling for mood.
> Quality, variety, and control of tone.
> Rhythmic impulse and phrasing.
> Observance of details and marks of expression.
> Pedalling at a suitable grade.

The choice of tempo can influence the whole performance for good or ill, and is much more important than many people realize.

We are dealing now with the performance of the piece as a whole, and are assuming that the preliminary learning of the notes, time, and detail has been accomplished.

The experienced artist will choose the tempo at which he feels the composer intended the piece to be played. In this he is guided by the indication given above, such as andante, allegro, and so on. Within the limits of these indications he brings his own feelings to bear, with the result that no two performances of a work will be exactly alike.

With the child pianist this is not quite so easy. He has to play within his own limitations. The tempo chosen must, in the first place, be one at which he knows he can play the piece throughout. The opening bars may be comparatively easy, and he romps through them cheerfully, undaunted by difficulties ahead. This, also, is the result of the many weeks it may have taken to learn the piece. He will have played the opening bars more than any other part of the piece, and there is about them a kind of familiarity that breeds contempt. It is not always easy for the pupil to see the piece as a whole. It is divided up in his mind into the bits he can play easily, and the parts he is not so happy about.

He should, of course, be taught to practise in the right way, resting the beginning and concentrating on the difficult parts, but he will still need help from the teacher to balance these parts up and to knit the piece into a whole.

It is a good thing for a complete performance of the piece to be given at each lesson, not necessarily by the pupil, but by the teacher continuing where the pupil leaves off. When the pupil reaches the second part, the process is reversed: the teacher plays the beginning, and the pupil continues where she leaves off. She must, of course, adapt her speed to that at which the pupil can continue. Again, it is very helpful for the teacher to play one hand, whilst the pupil plays the other throughout.

There are teachers who look upon the metronome with suspicion, and do not use it for teaching young pupils. If it were not for their high cost I should like all my pupils to possess one. It depends, of course, upon how it is used. No piece should be played to the metronome throughout, but the pupil should learn to use it for checking up the relative speeds of the various sections of a piece. It is a useful aid to the teacher when directing methods of practice. She might write in the notebook 'Practice bars 17 to 24 at M.M.

$\downarrow$ = 72. Gradually increase the speed at each practice, but not beyond M.M. $\downarrow$ = 100.' Here the pupil knows exactly what is expected of him.

Where the *composer* writes a metronome mark over the piece, we have a very clear idea as to how he intends it to go; but where the metronome marks are written by *editors* it is surprising what a variety of opinion there is, and it would be as well for the performer (provided he has the experience) to decide for himself how he feels he can best interpret the music. In this he is guided, as has already been mentioned, by indications of speed, such as allegro, andante, adagio, and so on.

These terms can be somewhat misleading, and in reading them, one must remember they refer to the speed of the *beats*, not of the notes. In this way a piece marked adagio can contain passages which need technical skill and speed.

Many students misinterpret the word 'andante' as meaning 'slow'. Its literal translation is 'walking', and it should be taken as 'moving along'. Again, it is not always realized that the speed of pieces in compound time is counted by the *beats*, *not their sub-divisions*, and that in 6/8 time, where there are two beats in a bar, a piece marked 'andante' would move along at quite a fair speed.

The word 'allegro' can denote a variety of speeds. In interpreting it the word 'lively' is given first consideration. Allegro, of course, means fast, but the rhythmic vitality and vigour of the performance are usually considered more important than speed of notes.

The child who has acquired a good technique is greatly tempted to rattle off everything at a great speed, thereby winning the admiration of his young friends at school, and possibly also of the people at home. Such children should be encouraged to listen to the performances of great artists. Radio and Television provide a tremendous choice of listening and the teacher could suggest special programmes, drawing attention to the poetic grandeur of a slow movement or the gentle beauty of a Chopin Nocturne. Such listening does much to awaken the appreciation of sensitive piano tone and the pupil soon learns that, even where a lively tempo is indicated, clarity and musical detail should never be overruled by sheer speed.

So it is, then, that we must carefully set the tempo for each piece. It could be described as the basic pulse. Within this basic pulse we get what might be called the artist's licence, his own personal feeling and self-expression—an elasticity of the time applied in a way that does not rob the music of its rhythmic impulse, but saves it from the monotony of metronomic precision. This 'rubato' is impossible to teach to those who cannot *feel* it, and, in any case, would not be taught in the earlier stages, though the musical child will develop a feeling for it after a term or two.

It is an indisputable fact that the average pianist is inclined to hurry when he reaches a quick passage, and drag the time when he reaches a slow passage. Of these two, the hurrying is the most persistent, especially in moments of nervous excitement, such as at public performances. The remedy for this is in the hands of the performer, though practice with a metronome can help up to a point. Passages where the *fingers* are inclined to 'run away' should be practised at a slower speed with a variety of accentuation. Where it is the *brain* that runs away, the performer needs to rehearse as often as possible in front of an audience, even if it be an audience of only one person!

Before a public performance, however simple the piece, the pianist should sit quietly for a second or two, and 'feel' the speed at which he is going to begin, mentally playing the first few bars. I am reminded of the famous conductor who, at a rehearsal, stood before his orchestra, his baton poised ready to begin, and then, before one note had been played, suddenly dropped his arms and said: 'No, too fast'.

The tempo chosen must, of course, be the correct one to convey the character and mood of the music. Mood is largely a matter of personal feeling, and the ability of the performer to convey what he feels. This ability depends on that rather intangible quality which is sometimes described as 'getting it across to the audience', and is also qualified by the technical and tonal control the pianist has at his command.

Let us go back once more to the very young pupil. We will imagine that he is to play a piece called 'March of the Soldiers'. The piece opens in the left hand, with the beat of the drums and the tramp of feet, thus:

These chords need a firm, crisp touch to convey the effect that is required, and the way in which they are played 'sets the stage' for the piece. Again, we have another piece, this time 'The March of the Shadow Men' and, by a strange co-incidence, it begins with the same chords in the left hand. But here they will have to be played quite differently: there is something mysterious and furtive about them. The men are creeping along almost silently. The teacher can do much to stimulate the child's imagination by painting word-pictures of the way in which a bar or two is to be played.

Here are some opening bars for the right hand:

Supposing we call this 'The Whistling Errand-boy'. It needs to be played gaily, almost roughly, with plenty of accent and swing. Then again we will change the title to 'Tree-top tune'—the gentle song of the birds. What a different picture this paints! And any child will appreciate the difference between the two moods.

Now a 'Lullaby' is to be played—one that has a definite rocking rhythm. The child should imagine the gentle rocking of the baby as he plays it, and, if very small, might enjoy making the rocking movements while the teacher plays the piece.

So it is that in the very youngest performers a feeling for mood can be developed if the teacher will appeal to their imagination and train their fingers to interpret what they feel.

Now we must consider quality, variety, and control of tone. What a big and important subject this is! We begin to teach the pupil to listen for quality and variety at the very first lesson, and much has been said about these things already in this book. To produce the tone required, a pupil needs a sensitive ear, sensitive fingers, and a feeling for balance; but none of these qualities can be developed without good teaching. Above all else, the teacher should aim at giving her pupils a beautiful touch: they must learn to become masters of the instrument, to make it sing at their command, and to make it a means of self-expression. This is not so idealistic as many would think. One has only to listen to a number of children playing at an Examination or Festival Competition to pick out those who have been taught on these lines. They may not even be the most gifted or the most advanced, but the minute they are on the piano stool one can see, and hear, that they know what they intend to do.

I once read that the way to make a note sing is to have an 'intense desire to do so'.[1] This answer appeals to me very much. It is as though the brain sends a message to the finger, by way of the arm, and the message is just 'Sing'. I have often tried this suggestion on young pupils, particularly when one hand has to sing the melody whilst the other is accompanying, and it certainly does help. To make one hand sing more than the other is always difficult at first, and, in the long run, I am sure that it is the 'intense desire' to do it that wins through.

We do not need to wait for a piece requiring melody and accompaniment before trying this out. A lot of fun can be

[1] *Keys to the Keyboard.* Andor Foldes (O.U.P.).

had by playing either five-finger exercises or scales with one hand singing more than the other. It can be treated as a game, and the teacher must say which hand is supposed to be the singing one. It is usually found more difficult at first to bring the left hand into the foreground, but practice and perseverance will get results in the end.

Another way of practising melody and accompaniment is for the melody hand to play clearly whilst the accompanying hand only moves over the keys without depressing them. This can be quite a challenge, but soon we realize that some of the accompanying notes *are* of importance, so I do not recommend this as an habitual form of practice (see examples on page 138).

Later will come the necessity to be able to play one finger in a hand with a more singing tone than the others, especially where the melody is the top note of chords. The same principles apply.

Contrapuntal music is the best practice of all for independence of tone control. The two-part inventions of Bach are ideal, but these cannot usually be tackled during the first year or two. Unfortunately many educational albums that filled the gap are now out of print. I can only offer my recently published *Two of a Kind* (Forsyth). The pupil learns to think of his hands as two separate voices, and this is another place where, before the piece is finished, the teacher and pupil can play it as a duet, taking one hand each.

It is not, however, only a case of balance between the sounds that are played simultaneously, but of balance between notes played consecutively. Here we must realize that grading of tone is qualified and conditioned by the rhythmic impulse of the music, and that it is not possible to divide the different aspects of interpretation into water-tight compartments.

If the composer were to give written directions for every nuance of tone within each phrase, the page would be so

¹ *Beginning to Play the Piano.* Sidney Harrison (O.U.P.).

covered with marks of expression as to make the notes hardly legible. It is therefore assumed that the natural rhythmic sense of the performer will lead him to supply the tonal shadings. The child who does this shows that he has a sense of interpretation which is beginning to develop through rhythm.

The rhythmic sense leads us, first of all, to make the natural accent according to the time of the piece, and about which I wrote earlier in the book. It must be understood that this is a *natural* accent. Those who cannot 'feel' it, but only 'put it in' because they have been told, do so with such monotonous regularity that the music is completely killed, and the performance can only be likened to that of a well-timed machine in a factory. The intensity of this accent should vary from bar to bar, according to its position in the phrase and the mood of the music, and must not obtrude itself with a sudden bump into a graceful curved line of sound.

The accent is not, of course, the only thing which governs tonal shadings. The relative speed of one note with another is an important guiding factor. A semibreve, for instance, would require a stronger tone than a quaver. This is because it has to sing for a greater length of time, and, on the piano, there is always an immediate fading of sound after the note has been played. It would follow, for the same reason, that where a dotted crotchet is followed by a quaver the amount of tone given to the quaver should match the fading off of the dotted crotchet note:

Clementi

Looking at the same example, there is another point to be noticed where the three Gs are repeated. They should not all be played with exactly the same amount of tone. In this particular case the difference is only very slight, because none of the three comes on an accented beat, but the second G (which falls *on* a beat) should be given slightly more stress than the other two.

In brilliant passages, where quaver (or semiquaver) runs are to be taken at speed, and where the music is marked 'forte', it does not follow that each quaver should be played forte. The intensity of tone is, as it were, passed from one accented beat to another, the intervening quavers supplying the bridge which carries the ear onward, and giving the feeling of speed and brilliance.

Where the music is marked 'piano', this does not mean there should be no gradation of tone. Beginners are inclined to try to play too softly before they have sufficient control. Above all else, they must make the notes sing, and a nuance in the melody line is as essential in soft playing as in louder music.

This nuance of tone does not only apply to lines of melody. The accompanying hand, though less prominent than the melody, has its own rise and fall of tone. Again this is largely conditioned by the natural accent. The 'Alberti bass', which is frequently used by Haydn and Mozart, and which became almost a formula for Sonata or Sonatina writing during that period, needs very skilful handling. The young pianist, starting on the Sonatinas of Clementi or Kuhlau, can easily spirit all their charm away by a relentless 'churning away' at the left hand.

Here is a typical example of this kind of accompaniment:

Mozart Sonata in C. K 545

Any number of melodies còuld be written over this same bass (in a variety of keys), and the first thing to avoid is a heavy thumb. The constant reiteration of the dominant is a typical feature here, and this note must be played as softly as possible. Now, by careful study of the left-hand in relationship with the right-hand melody, there will emerge the structure, or 'shape', around which the quavers are built. This gives us the clue to the tonal nuance of the accompaniment.

It is a good plan to write this out in a manuscript book for the pupil to play, and at the same time take the first few bars of works of the same type for further illustration. I give one further example here:

Beethoven Sonatina in F

Followed by its 'skeleton structure':

So far I have not mentioned 'marks of expression' as written by the composer or editor. Some copies are more heavily edited than others, though, as I have already said, it would be impossible for the composer to indicate, by written marks, every shade of tone which the music demands. Let us suppose that the beginning of a piece similar to the last two examples is marked *mf*. To what does the *mf* refer? The right hand, the left hand, or both? Musical instinct tells us that it refers to the hand which has the melody, and that the accompaniment should, of course, be softer. This is only one case where a mark of expression cannot be taken literally.

The most misunderstood expression marks are the crescendo and diminuendo, particularly when they are represented by the following signs —————— ——————. The very shape of these leads the pupil into thinking that the notes within them either increase or decrease in tone one by one throughout the duration of the sign. Let us take as an example part of the little Beethoven Sonatina I have just quoted:

The impression given is that the E at the bottom of the run is the softest note, but in actual fact, coming on the first beat of the bar, it is not as soft as the semiquavers that precede it. The diminuendo is carried from beat to beat rather than from note to note.

Now we look at the bar that follows: the melody climbs up once more in a crescendo. C is the climax, and B flat 'floats off' with sufficient tone to match the fading of the C. But the left-hand semiquavers are not increased in tone from first to last—the 'in between' notes are played softly, the crescendo being observed by those notes that form the harmonic structure.

As a final illustration I cannot do better than quote an idea once suggested to me by Sidney Harrison. He asks his pupil to repeat the words 'Louder and *Louder* and LOUDER'. Here

it is discovered that the loudest note in this example is not
the last:

This shows us that expression is a matter of rhythm and
accentuation, and can only be partly indicated on the printed
page. It is for the pianist to read into the composer's inten-
tions according to the dictates of the rhythmic and melodic
line of the music.

In everything that concerns the performance of the piece,
the detailed interpretation of each written sign is, in the end,
left to the performer. For instance, the composer will indicate that certain notes are to be played staccato. There are
varying degrees of staccato, and signs approximating to each
degree. These are:

1.   ♩̇   = The shortest possible sound, or staccatissimo.

2.   ♩̇   = Normal staccato, still short and sharp.

3.   ♩̄   = Less short, though still detached.

4.   ♩ ♩ = Much the same as the above, but less accented.
         This is often found in slow music where pedal
         is to be used.

These signs, however, are seldom found in the large
majority of editions. In many cases No. 2 is used to cover all
degrees of staccato, though No. 4 will frequently be found in
slow movements of classical sonatas and music of a similar
type. It will be seen, therefore, that a great deal is left to the
judgement of the performer as to the degree of shortness

which should be given to each note. Here again it is a matter of experience, and the teacher will have to indicate these differences in the early stages.

The same applies to accents. In some works a sudden intensity of sound is intended—Beethoven was very fond of these violent dynamics—in others there should be a slight accentuation. Composers have made attempts to differentiate between these with such signs as – > ∧ *sf* but, unfortunately, there are no uniform rules about them.

The pause is another sign that requires good judgement to produce exactly the right effect. The length of the pause depends on the proportion of the music. By that I mean that a big work having grand and impressive climaxes could stand longer pauses than a short piece of very slight structure.

All these details are conditioned again by the instrument, the acoustics of the room, and, even, the responsiveness of the audience. Not only do two performers rarely play the same pieces in the same way, but one individual will give a different interpretation of the same piece on separate occasions.

In teaching these things a great deal of thought and care must go into such details. The various methods of performance should be demonstrated by the teacher, and a reason given for the choice of tempo, style, variations of the staccato, accent, and other details. As the pupil gains in experience, his opinion should be asked, and, where it is at all possible, his own ideas should go into any work he is studying.

My sixth heading on page 129 is 'Pedalling', but there is no need to write about it here, as a chapter has been devoted to it earlier in the book, to which the reader can refer.

The young pianist begins to give a performance the moment his mind is concerned with the sound rather than with the notes. Through the process of listening and self-criticism he will be on the way to giving an interpretation. It is for the teacher to bring him up to have an appreciation for the finer details of performance. Interpretation is, in the end, an individual and personal thing; it is an act of self-expression; but there are such things as 'good taste' and 'bad taste' in performance, and this is where the early teaching counts more than anything else.

SPECIAL OCCASIONS

THE average child loves a special occasion. It is all part of the exciting experience of life, and will be talked about for days beforehand. Later he will lose some of the supreme self-confidence of childhood and become self-critical and apprehensive, but if he has had some experience of playing in public in the early years, it will help him considerably in the future.

It should be taken as a matter of course that the child who is learning the piano will play to people without any fuss, and that there is nothing out of the ordinary in being asked to do so. The teacher can help in this respect by seeing that—after the initial stages—the pupil always has something that he can play, however short and simple it may be. When a piece is known it should be kept up, so that a miniature repertoire is built up. The pupil can give a few minutes once or twice a week to his old pieces, which are only dropped as others come along to fill their places. One get so tired of hearing the excuse that a child has forgotten his last piece and doesn't know the new one yet. The teacher is largely to blame for this, and should make a point of giving a little time every now and then to revising the repertoire.

(1) CONCERTS

The concert can vary from an informal affair at home to something on quite a grand scale, with party dresses and printed programmes. Whatever the occasion, this has to be a performance, and artistic standards are aimed at. Most children respond well if they have something special for which to work, and will make an extra effort which has a good effect on their general progress. The very shy child is rare these days, but, of course, no child should be *forced* to play in public.

It is most important that the concert piece is well within the ability of the performer. The child should be competely confident that he can manage the notes, so that he can give thought to the music and *how* it should be played. A margin must be allowed for nervous excitement, and if the piece is too difficult it will mean a double strain on the nerves, which will result in a hesitant performance and often a breakdown. This sort of thing undermines the child's confidence and makes any future occasions a source of dread to him. It gives more pleasure to the audience to hear a simple piece played with obvious enjoyment and understanding than to sit through the agonized struggles of one whose work is far too difficult. At the end a sigh of relief is breathed because he 'got through it'; but music is not meant to be 'got through'!

The choosing of the concert piece, then, is vitally important, and endless trouble should be taken to give each pupil something that suits him musically and technically, and that he enjoys playing. Duets and, if possible, works for two pianos make excellent concert items. Apart from the musical experience gained, they add variety to the programme, and performers who are inclined to be nervous are much more at ease if playing with someone else.

The young artist should learn something about platform deportment. One does not want to see affectation, or overexaggerated mannerisms, but he should be taught not to rush on and off the stage as though the whole thing had to be got over as quickly as possible. It is a good thing to practise this as part of the performance, remembering to approach the piano without turning his back on the audience, and to see that the stool is the right height and the correct distance from the keyboard when he is seated. There should be just sufficient pause for him to remember the tempo and mood of the piece before it is started. Of course, with very young children, these things are only learnt gradually, and the teacher (or someone appointed) should be at hand to see to them. Even small pupils should practise coming on and off, and remember not to rise from the stool whilst still clutching the keys with their fingers. This is the commonest fault of all in the very young. The pupil also must practise the bow— not a very easy achievement! It usually turns into either an abrupt duck of the head or a complicated affair in which the child hugs his tummy in imitation of the old courtly style. If possible, we want a happy medium between these two. Where there are no printed programmes, and the music has to be announced, let it be done in a simple and straightfor-ward manner—just the title and the composer. I have seen children strike a pose worthy of a prima donna, and announce in a dramatic way: 'I am now going to play for you . . .' After such a sensational announcement the playing seldom comes up to expectations!

Mothers can be a trial before or during concerts, mainly because the child's appearance is often more important to them than his performance. The teacher should take the greatest trouble to see that each performer *is* looking his (or her) best. To avoid confusion, I have had to refer to the pupil as 'He' throughout the book, but I feel I must, at this moment, stress the importance of 'hair-dos' for little girls, whilst boys always seem to need 'straightening out' before going on to perform. The mother will never feel the concert has been a success if these things are not in order. One can look around the audience and pick out the parents of the performer by the look either of pride or anxiety on their faces, but if a child is not properly turned out the look may turn to one of fury, accompanied by angry mutterings. So let the teacher beware!

Now we come to the young artist who is older and more experienced, and takes the whole affair more seriously from the musical point of view. He needs confidence more than the small child, because he is only too conscious of his short-comings. If the work he has to play has been well chosen and learnt, the teacher will be able to make him realize that there is nothing to worry about. It should be stressed that small slips and wrong notes do not matter, provided the performance conveys the meaning of the music.

If the concert is to be held in a strange hall it is best to try to arrange a rehearsal there. The younger pupils will then feel more at home in the new surroundings, and the more advanced pupils will get a chance to get the feel of the keys, to test the depth and response of the pedals, and to gauge the tonal qualities of the piano in relationship to the size of the room. It must be remembered that the acoustics of a room change considerably when it is full of people, and that much of the resonance is lost. The student will probably notice an echoing or a slight blurring in a large empty hall, but must be told that when the audience is there everything will sound more clear cut, and he may even need to add more resonance to his own performance.

Then there is the question of playing from memory. Beginners often do this more easily than advanced performers, because they have learnt largely by rote, or by the constant repetition of a short piece. In the later stages memory becomes more a matter of individual ability, and it is not always the best pianists who memorize the most easily. A slow learner will memorize a piece through having to play it so many times, and this form of muscular memory is developed by many young pianists. It only remains reliable so long as there is complete confidence and absence of nerves. Once the pianist starts wondering what the next note is, and tries to bring his mind as well as his fingers to the question, he will hesitate and be lost, with little chance of anything but a complete stop. Frantically he goes back to the beginning, but this time the mind is at work, and probably the same thing will happen again at the same place.

The quick learner who grasps the music at a glance repeats

the piece fewer times whilst learning it, and only needs to give the extra repetition to the passages that are technically difficult. He has to develop a memory which relies on a musical knowledge of the piece, its progressions and harmonies. This takes time and concentration, and, often, he would rather play with the music there for reference, than spend many extra hours memorizing it, in which he could otherwise be studying something new. There is no doubt that a performance from memory makes a better visual impression on the audience, but some of the finest playing I have ever heard has been from young pianists who have had the music there, though giving it only the merest glance occasionally. They have been able to give themselves wholeheartedly to the music, without a small nagging at the back of their minds that memory may fail.

It must be remembered that I am not writing about professional musicians, but about young people who are still at school, and have a multitude of other things to fill their minds and brains. I do feel most strongly that they should not be forced to memorize, but to be allowed to play in the way that they feel they can best do justice to the music.

So, then, let all those who can play by heart at the concert do so, for it is an excellent thing, but do not let us badger anyone into doing it who has any doubts at all. Teach how to memorize in lessons, teach the formation of the chords and progressions that occur in the piece: but do not force the pupil to go through agonies at a public performance, or make comparisons between those who play from memory and those who do not. If anyone has hopes of being a virtuoso pianist he will know only too well that his memory must be developed, for public opinion to-day demands it, and only the well-known and established pianists can risk taking the book on to the platform without a surprised comment from the critics.

The concert is an excellent experience, and teaches children to take an interest in the performance of others. They will sometimes arrive at their next lesson fired with enthusiasm to play like 'So-and-so', and this gives them a new aim in their piano-playing, and results in harder work.

(2) EXAMINATIONS

Not every pupil is a suitable examination candidate, and unless examinations can be taken without bother and fuss it is better that they should not be attempted. To many, however, they act as a stimulus to hard work, and help to bring all branches of their studies on a level, so that the weaker points (sight-reading, aural tests, &c) are given more thought and care.

A pupil should take exams in his stride, and should be reasonably near the required standard before the examination pieces are begun. To give a child an examination book at the beginning of the year, in the hopes that he will have struggled to somewhere near the standard by the end of the year, is the wrong way to set about it. Examinations prepared for in this way are usually abandoned, or else are taken with not very gratifying results. The pupil is lucky if he scrapes through, and I have even heard one proud parent boast to another: 'My Johnny only failed his exam by three marks'. In actual fact Johnny must really have played very badly to have failed at all; or was it that everything except the pieces had been woefully neglected? Of course, the usual excuse for failure is 'nerves'. But I cannot agree that nerves are ever the *only* reason for failure; there *must* be other contributing factors. The first and foremost of these is that the work is not sufficiently well known to allow for accidents of any kind. It must be terrifying to enter the examination room knowing that one is completely unsafe from the start. The knowledge is enough to fail the candidate before he ever enters the room. Examiners are kindly people, and most of them have spent many years in giving a sympathetic ear to candidates of all ages. They are there to find the good in the performance, not to jump triumphantly on anything which is bad. From their experience they can tell whether shakiness or even a temporary breakdown is due to nerves. They are not primarily concerned with wrong notes, or occasional slips. They are seeking for a musical and purposeful performance that conveys the spirit and mood of the music and care for phrasing and detail. The pulse, too, must be alive yet steady—not varying according to the difficulty of the passages! A lot can be forgiven if these things are evident. The following true story will illustrate my point.

Some years ago two little girls took their first examination. We will call them Mary and Frances. Mary was a self-possessed young lady, quite a safe examination candidate, but with little imagination and a very 'solid' approach to the piano. Frances was less safe, perhaps; but there was a rare quality about her playing that turned the simplest phrase into a thing of real beauty; music spoke a language to her, which she expressed even at this early stage. After the examination was over they were, of course, surrounded by a group of friends, who eagerly asked: 'What was it like? How did you get on? Was he nice?' 'Well,' replied Mary, 'I got on all right, but Frances didn't.' 'What happened?' asked the children. Frances, looking rather crestfallen, seemed unwilling to reply, so Mary explained, 'Frances says she played some *wrong notes* and she did it more than once.' Now that the awful truth was out, Frances found her tongue. 'He was very nice,' she said, 'and didn't say anything about them, but I am afraid I have failed.' In due course the results arrived. Mary had a good pass and Frances had gained Distinction.

This story will call for comment on the comparison between the naturally gifted child and her less gifted but harder-working friend. I am afraid this is a case where we cannot get away from facts. The naturally artistic child will always make a better musician than another who is less imaginative and sensitive: but only a very small percentage of children are devoid of artistic sense, and it is surprising how it can be developed through the medium of the piano, if the teaching is directed towards these ideals.

Then, of course, we get the more practical side of the examination, scales, and broken chords or arpeggios. No one can do well if these are not known, and there seems no reason not to know them if they have been carefully prepared. They will have been included in each lesson, whether an examination is being taken or not, and it must never be left until a few weeks before the exam for the pupil to be told exactly which will be expected. During the previous term a list should be made of those that will be required. Any that are already known will be ticked, and those which are new will be carefully taught one by one, each one being ticked when it can be played perfectly, and put on the 'revision' list. Those that are to be revised can be listed at so many a day, to make sure they are regularly practised. The teacher, at each lesson, will hear some from the revision list, and, of course, the new one, which must be written in detail in the notebook, its key signature and its chord being understood at the same time. Broken chords and arpeggios should be taught in the same way.

In a previous chapter I have talked about sight-reading, and here again the tests of the required Grade should not be left until the last minute, but gradually worked up during the previous term. Aural tests are difficult to fit into all piano lessons, and many of them can be taken in class at school. For those who have not this advantage the teacher must make a point of regular practice, not just before the examination, but a little at each lesson. The pupil must have clearly in his mind exactly what will be expected of him.

The set pieces should not be given too early. Two terms at the most should be sufficient for studying them if the pupil is up to the Grade. Two of them might be learnt the term before the examination and one during the examination term, to allow plenty of time for a final polish. It is difficult to have three pieces up to 'concert pitch' all at the same time, and those that are first learnt should be given a rest occasionally, so that they do not become stale. If the pupil has become bored with a piece it will be evident in his performance of it, and care has to be exercised to try not to let this happen. Any music that requires technical agility can very quickly get out of hand once it has been learnt. Children love to play quickly and cannot resist playing at a rate over which they have no control. Slow practice will have to be insisted upon, or, if the piece has fallen to pieces, a week's rest, followed by a daily dose of slow practice even after the cure has been completed.

The pupil should be ready a week before the first possible examination date, and spend any time that remains in learning something fresh, and in sight-reading anything which takes his fancy, leaving examination music to be played through on alternate days.

This, of course, is the ideal; but unfortunately the best-laid plans sometimes go astray. Pupils may be absent for several weeks, or suffer from one of those extraordinary lapses which seem to occur *after* the entry has been sent in. Out of every dozen candidates, perhaps *one* will need all the teacher's patience and help. It may mean hard and persistent work, and the teacher feels that she is literally dragging the pupil along, but there are few children who will not be galvanized into action by a really determined and enthusiastic teacher. There are people who will say: 'Why worry about those who do not work? they do not deserve to pass.' Fortunately for the child, most teachers have too much professional pride to allow this to happen, and they feel that it is their failure if the pupil loses interest. There is also the child's future to consider. After all, music examinations do not *have* to be taken: but, if they are, there is nothing to be gained, and everything to be lost, in failing them. The child loses confidence, the teacher loses prestige, and the parents lose the examination fee.

In the ordinary way no extra lessons should be necessary The less fuss the better. At the last lesson before the examination there should be as little adverse criticism and as much praise and encouragement as possible. What is not right by then is very unlikely to be improved at the last minute. It is fatal to send the pupil away with a string of admonitions not to forget this, that, or the other. Much better to say: 'Well now, you've nothing to worry about. Enjoy yourself and try to make the examiner enjoy your playing. I am sure that everything will go well.'

On the day of examination do not 'fuss' the candidate. I have seen and heard children being treated as though they were semi-invalids on such occasions. If the examination is being held in the school, no one should be sent for until ten minutes before he is to enter the room. This will give time for a wash and a tidy up, but will not mean a long wait: there is no point in arriving hours before the appointed time.

For many years my house has been used as a centre for the Associated Board, and I have had candidates waiting as much as an hour. This cannot always be avoided where a group arrives together; but if this is likely to happen, those who are waiting should be kept occupied with books or magazines that really interest them, or, where possible, sent out in the garden, or for a walk.

These, then, are the most important points to remember:

Make sure that a child is reasonably near the required Grade before giving an examination book.

Make it absolutely clear to the pupil what will be expected.

Practise scales, arpeggios, sight-reading, and aural tests regularly and systematically.

Train the pupil to give a musical interpretation of the set pieces and not worry over slips at the examination.

Make the pupil feel that you have confidence in his ability to do well.

(3) FESTIVALS

To enter for a Competitive Festival a child must have reached a fairly good standard for his age. Unless the set piece is well within his capabilities, it should not be attempted. Far more is required than mere note-playing, and nothing can be gained by allowing someone who is below standard to enter. The experience will be nerve-racking for the child and do the teacher no good. It is pathetic to hear some of the performances that are given at these Festivals, and even more pathetic to see the child's face if he comes in for some unfavourable criticism. In such a case no one can be blamed but the teacher. It is a poor excuse to say that the parents insisted he should enter. Far better to stand up to them, and if necessary lose the pupil, than to lower one's standard and reputation. Of course, all competitors make mistakes, and all come in for criticism, but sheer inefficiency is unmistakable. I remember, not so long ago, hearing a most helpful and painstaking adjudicator give a short criticism to every member of a large piano class. When he came to a certain little boy, he said: 'Now, I am afraid this won't do at all. Either the piece is too difficult for you, or you have not been shown how to play it.' Imagine what the small boy must have felt like! It was not his fault. He had no standard to judge himself by until he had heard the others. It must have made him, and his parents, completely lose faith in the teacher, and really she deserved it. Neither was he a complete exception. There were others equally bad. This is where a teacher must realize her responsibility, and not allow her standard to lapse, or allow children to think that any kind of performance will do so long as they can put on their most attractive dress (girls again!), and play to a real audience. Incidentally, those who are the most simply dressed and have the quietest platform manners usually turn out to be the musicians.

In contrast to these terrible performances are those by the really brilliant children, who become a byword at any Festival. The teacher who has such pupils must be careful that their attitude towards competitions does not become one of 'pot hunting'. Where there is obviously no one of their standard likely to compete, it would be better not to enter for classes confined to their own age-groups, especially after they have reached the age of thirteen or fourteen. Most Festivals provide a number of special classes to attract these talented young people—Sonata Classes, Repertoire Classes, Bach Classes, Concerto Classes, and so on. Most of these have a wider age range, and give the brilliant ones a chance of meeting together and really testing their powers. It is remarkable what a friendly spirit is usually found in these classes. Teachers of the 'stars' meet, and congratulate each other on their progress since last year, the competitors themselves get together and compare notes, or clap each other heartily on the back while they swallow their own disappointment. Of course, they all cherish a secret hope that they may win, but far more important is the spirit in which they compete, and the experience gained. Where there is real musicianship they are generous in their admiration of one another, and it is only occasionally that hard feeling crops up. Parents are more often guilty of this than competitors, owing to a natural partiality for their own offspring! Here is another case where the teacher needs more than just a musical training if she is to keep parents as well as competitors calm and unruffled. She certainly needs to display these qualities herself and to hide any personal feelings she may have on the matter.

Between the two extremes of good and bad comes the large majority of competitors who are the backbone of the Festival. They are the ones that really prove their teacher's worth. No teacher can be judged better than by listening to those of her pupils who might be described as 'good average'. One can pick out those who have been well taught immediately they begin to play. Even nerves and wrong notes cannot hide the evidence. The difference lies in all those little things about which I have written so fully in the chapters 'Common Faults and their Prevention' and 'The Pathway to Performance'. To say here exactly how to prepare a pupil for a Festival would be simply to repeat all that again, and I can offer no further suggestions beyond a reminder that a good

platform deportment is an advantage. Of course, there is no
need to announce the piece (unless it is an 'own choice' and
the competitor is requested to do so), nor should there be a
bow at the end, but a business-like approach to the work
usually precedes a good performance. Competitors who rush
on and off invariably rush through their pieces as well. Often
the competitor may have to wait for some time until the
adjudicator is ready. More than 90 per cent of the smaller
children, and indeed many of the bigger ones too, sit clutching the keyboard, with their fingers ready over the first notes.
When the bell goes, or the adjudicator asks them to begin,
they go off like a shot from a gun. This cannot have a very
settling effect on the rhythm of the opening bars. It would be
far better to wait with their hands in their laps until the time
to begin, and then pause for a minute to feel the rhythm before beginning. The adjudicator will like this much better
than the 'shotgun' method. A sense of repose while waiting
is not a very easy thing for young people to acquire, and
should be practised during the lesson, the teacher acting as
adjudicator.

Classes are usually arranged for such things as ensemble
playing, sight-reading, accompaniment, and general musicianship. Duet-playing is particularly good for the younger
competitors, who learn a lot about 'give and take', and are
able to hear its effects in other performances. Older students
should be encouraged to enter for all kinds of ensemble work
and for classes that call for individual initiative and general
musical intelligence.

When the day of the competition arrives the competitor
can be saved a great deal of nervous strain if the parents and
teacher will treat the whole affair in as everyday a manner
as possible. Before the child goes up to play all that is
needed is a word of encouragement and confidence, and on
no account streams of last minute 'Do's and Don't's'. Some
children will notice that the piece is performed at many
different speeds and in different ways, but they must be made

to realize that the way they have practised it is the way in which they can play it best. Experience has proved that the quickest performance is seldom the most successful.

Music Festivals of the non-competitive type do not often arrange classes for piano, which is a pity, as certain children would benefit from the non-competitive atmosphere. However, the Competitive Festival has done much to raise the standard of piano-playing throughout the country. Its value lies in the helpful criticisms given by the adjudicator, and in the experience of listening to other performances. The teacher, more than anyone else, can build up her experience and add to her ideas through attending Piano Classes at Festivals, whether she has entered pupils for them or not.

CONCLUSION

THE wonderful thing about teaching is the ever-growing experience that it gives us, and in writing this I can but offer my experience up to the present. This has extended over a number of years, during which I have dealt with every age and Grade, from four-year-olds to Diploma students. If I could take a census of a thousand pupils, I could honestly say that no two have been alike, or have presented the same problems. It is an alertness to these problems and an appreciation of human nature that make the successful teacher.

I do most sincerely hope that the ideas set forth here will be of use to those who belong to my profession, and to whom I wish as much happiness in it as I have found.